Fab Friends and Best Buds

Real Girls on Making Forever Friends

Erika V. Shearin Karres, Ed.D.

Adams Media
Avon, Massachusetts

Copyright ©2005, Erika V. Shearin Karres, Ed.D.
All rights reserved. This book, or parts thereof, may not be reproduced in any form without permission from the publisher; exceptions are made for brief excerpts used in published reviews.

Published by
Adams Media, an F+W Publications Company
57 Littlefield Street, Avon, MA 02322. U.S.A.
www.adamsmedia.com

ISBN: 1-59337-293-0

Printed in Canada.

J I H G F E D C B A

Library of Congress Cataloging-in-Publication Data
Karres, Erika V. Shearin.
Fab friends and best buds / Erika V. Shearin Karres.
p. cm.
ISBN 1-59337-293-0
1. Teenage girls—Juvenile literature. 2. Friendship in adolescence—Juvenile literature. 3. Female friendship—Juvenile literature. I. Title.
HQ798.K353 2005
302.3'4'08352—dc22
2005009562

This publication is designed to provide accurate and authoritative information with regard to the subject matter covered. It is sold with the understanding that the publisher is not engaged in rendering legal, accounting, or other professional advice. If legal advice or other expert assistance is required, the services of a competent professional person should be sought.

—From a *Declaration of Principles* jointly adopted by a Committee of the American Bar Association and a Committee of Publishers and Associations

Many of the designations used by manufacturers and sellers to distinguish their products are claimed as trademarks. Where those designations appear in this book and Adams Media was aware of a trademark claim, the designations have been printed in initial capital letters.

This book is available at quantity discounts for bulk purchases.
For information, please call 1-800-872-5627.

Dedication

THIS BOOK IS FOR Elizabeth S. Hounshell and Dr. Mary D. Shearin, my daughters and fab friends, and for Andrew M. Karres, my husband and best bud, with all my love and thanks.

Also for June Clark, my visionary literary agent.

And for Danielle Chiotti, my editor at Adams Media. Not only is Danielle a truly fab friend and best bud to those close to her, but also she's the same way to all girls and wishes them so well. Actually, Danielle goes beyond the wishing. She makes the wish a reality. With this book she shows every girl in the world how to have tons of terrific friends and live a great life, a wow life. In short, the best life possible.

Plus, those friendship lessons learned early will spawn a happy harvest in the years to come. Once grown up, the girls will become productive leaders and change agents in their communities and countries, and encourage their friends to do the same. Then, as a force of girlfriends working together, they will rule, and right the wrongs.

So, on behalf of girls everywhere now and in the future: Thank you, Danielle Chiotti! You're our role and soul model.

Contents

Acknowledgments

A VERY SPECIAL THANKS to all the girls who participated in my research and to my thoughtful teen readers, reviewers, advisers, and real-life experts. And to their parents.

And to Bettina Grahek, an excellent education leader; to Laura O'Brien, outstanding teacher; and to A. J. Gregory, a fab fellow researcher and writer. All three work hard every day to improve our world.

And to the numerous teachers who offered input and helped gather materials on this important topic. Now your fine work lives on not only in the academic achievements of your students, but also in the ever-widening ripples in the friendship ocean that this book will generate. From this moment on, your hard work is immortalized.

Your influence is forever.

Introduction
First Words

Are You There But Nowhere?

Hey there, girl! Do you know that you're at the most wonderful part of your life? Has it sunk in yet that you're really there—at the starting point of *everything*? Yes, this is the time . . .

- When lots of things are beginning to make more sense to you—at school, at home, and everywhere else!
- When you can do so much more than you used to, and
- When you finally get to enjoy more freedom!

Oh yeah, you know it. You can, like, feel it. Your whole life is about to change, pick up the tempo, and really get going. It's, like, you're finally getting *there*—where you always dreamed you'd be.

So what's the one thing you need to make this way incredible time in your life even better?

Friends.

> Without friends nothing is fun, but with friends even the worst is the best.
>
> Karyn, 17

You bet, Karyn. Hanging with your friends and chilling at will, spilling harmless secrets and laughing over so many silly things is probably a major part of your life. Right?

> Getting together with all my fab friends is way cool.
>
> Tina, 16

And the greatest part is—you get to hang with your friends every day—at school, at home, or at the mall. It makes life *so* exciting.

Being with my friends makes me feel like I'm in a movie.

Jennifer, 15

And even if you can't *see* all your pals every single day, then you can still exchange the latest info with them or confide in them in other ways. Yeah, you chat on the phone. You instant message over the Internet. You text them. Or sometimes you even do it the old-fashioned way—you write your bud a note and stick it in her locker. Sure, there are all kinds of ways to connect with your friends.

I make my friends my no. 1 priority and they do the same for me.

Brianne, 17

Right. Your friends really are the most important people in your life! They get you and you get them. They accept you just as you are, even on a bad hair day—especially on a bad hair day. Face it, right now you can't imagine life without your friends.

My friends are the greatest thing I have.

Kristi, 18

But what what if you lose them? For instance, what if:

- Your best friend moves and you miss her so, so much? Or you move?
- She joins a club you don't belong to and can't because you're no good at horseback riding. Those big beasts scare you!
- She finds a bunch of "cooler" buddies?
- The class hottie develops a crush on her and she disses you? What then?

Wouldn't you feel like you could just die?

Hey, if you've ever felt this way, no one can blame you. The power of friendship is amazing and the lack of friends can really, really hurt. But friendship can be sooo confusing. One moment you think you know who your friends are and what makes those chicks tick. Next, the girls you know aren't at all what you thought they were. Maybe they just don't treat you right or maybe they've changed. Or maybe they never were what you thought they were.

Sometimes great chicks turn into way mean chicks.

Andrea, 14

Okay, let's stop right here. So, what happens if you have a friend falling-out? What should you do? How should you act?

Once I understood what *real* friends are and how *real* friends treat you, I was, like, on top of the world. But it took me ages and ages.

Jamila, 18

No need to fear—you're going to get the real scoop on friends and friendship *now.*

The thing is to know what's a friend and what's a waste of time.

Mei Mei, 15

Yes. That's why you're reading this. Because you'll find out all about the kinds of friendship potential other girls have. You'll get the scoop on how to make supersmart decisions when it comes to your friends. Like, what types of girls are hopeless as friends, and what types of girls are happening chicks.

Having lots of friends is way, way crucial. They make you really live.

Serena, 18

Plus, en route to those many friends (and the best kinds meant just for you!), you'll get to take all sorts of fun tests to check yourself for your *own* friendship potential. Maybe that's something you haven't even thought about. But well, maybe there's this little turnoff about you that's been keeping you from finding all the fab friends just waiting out there for you. But now, you'll find out how to turn this turnoff into a *turn-on* for friends.

And into a super friend finder.

For that's the best part of this book. Page by page, you'll find out how you can become a major magnet and attract the girls with the most friendship talent as your fab friends, as your true friends, as your forever friends. And the amazing thing is that the friendly advice you get on every page comes directly from girls just like yourself. So, it's told like it is—real and honest, warts and all.

Trust me: The girls who have oodles of friends all over will tell you what they did to get them. They can't wait.

> I want to pass on all my friendship secrets.
>
> Tracie, 17

And the girls who have zero friends also want to talk to you. Beginning right this minute, they'll tell you what they did wrong.

> Oh, I wish so bad somebody had, like, clued me in before I made all those dumb friendship mistakes in school.
>
> Chloe, 19

Well, making lots of friendship mistakes won't happen to you. No, you'll avoid them and end up with all the top friendship secrets straight from the mouths of the insiders. You'll be way, way ahead.

Wow.

Let's start the process now!

The Expert

Ever since I immigrated to this country four decades ago, I've worked with young people in various capacities—as a teacher and mother, as an adviser, as a life coach, and now as the girl guru. So, I have lots of experience with girls like you. And I want to help you find all of the right tools you need to survive and thrive, especially today, because you have so much potential.

But you need more to soar. And by the time you finish this book, you'll be well on your way!

Girls Everywhere

I asked hundreds and hundreds of girls everywhere—girls in malls, in schools, and in class: What do you need to know to grow into the best you can be? And this is what they said, each and every one of them: "Friends." How can I help? I asked.

Give us a friendship survival guide! Please! We want plenty of good friends and lotsa best buds. This is the most important thing to us—friendship.

> The difference between having friends and not having them is like day and night.
>
> Brandi, 15

Sure, all the girls I talked to admitted that you can get along without friends. You can make it—if you absolutely have to.

But wow! What a great big difference it is when you have friends. Great friends, fabulous friends, best buddies. When you snag a few great chicks as your pals. That'll do the trick—every time. They make all the tough stuff easy, all the hurtful moments less hurtful. All the boring times, the best of times.

So, you see, having friends is way crucial.

That's why this friend-finding guide came about.

It was written *just for you*.

> Good friends are like family. They love you for who you are and wouldn't ask you to change unless it's for the best. Good friends will never hurt you. And they'll be there for you forever.
>
> Jessica, 17

Part 1
Faux Friends

n., pl.: Hard-to-fix chicks, problematic chicks, or better-nix-'em-quick chicks

You know the word *faux*. It means "fraud" or "fake" or "phony," like fake fur and faux pearls, which are man-made. Yeah, fake can be a good thing in your wardrobe, but not in relationships.

In friendship, fake means false, a sham, a dud, a disaster. In other words, the absolute worst. And believe me, you do not want fake friends! Not now, not ever. Fake friends are total phonies, and some are mean besides. So, be careful.

> These girls I know always say to one of their friends: At the mall could you, like, walk a few steps behind us? We don't wanna be seen walking with an ugly person.
>
> Doriss, 14

How mean is that? And they call themselves friends!

But even without a mean streak as wide as the Mississippi, there are girls, and quite a few of them, who don't have stellar friend potential. It could be for a lot of reasons—like their background, their immaturity, or circumstances and causes beyond their control.

> Worse than not having any friends is having fake friends acting like they're your real friends. Yeah, right. Watch your back, is all I have to say. Watch your back!
>
> Emily, 18

But how can you tell? First, by knowing all about the types of Faux Friends that are out there. Then, by being able to recognize them ASAP and from miles away. And finally, by protecting yourself from becoming a Faux Friend yourself!

If you hang around fakey chicks too much, it rubs off on you, so don't. Okay?

Suzan, 18

Now, just because we're talking about Faux Friends in this section, it doesn't mean that these girls are no good at all. It never means that! All girls are worthy of our respect. It's just that some girls are missing a little something. Most likely it's not their fault. Maybe their mom or dad wasn't there enough for them when they were small. But as a result, they are never sure they can totally count on somebody. They haven't developed a solid trust ability. So, their friendship ability is way low.

You know about the IQ, don't you? That's the intelligence quotient (amount or ability) some researchers established a long time ago. And maybe you've heard about the EQ, the emotional intelligence amount that some other researchers have recently discovered.

Well, what we're interested in here is the FQ, the *friendship quotient*. You need to know what the actual friendship quotient of the girls you know is. That's the quantity and quality of their being able to be a good friend to you, like we said.

And that's so important. Wow, and how.

It's best to hang with nice girls who treat you good, you know.

Page, 17

Here's the bonus: From this moment on, as you learn to see other girls as potential friends, you get a chance to get to know yourself. Whom you end up with as friends tells a whole lot about *you*.

Never, ever copy what the worst girls in school do. They might accept you with open arms, but what good is that when you've lowered yourself? Are you looking for future cellmates or college roommates?

Kelly Ann, 19

And in the process of becoming empowered to pick and choose the very best friends just right for you, you'll pick up all kinds of pointers too, so your own FQ can rise dramatically. You'll learn to power up your own friendship ability to the nth degree and then you'll be able to be a good friend. A better friend. No, a best friend forever to all kinds of superchicks.

What a good deal. This is so exciting!

> Friends who stab you in the back or do something to take you down or lie about you can scar you for life. It's like getting acne scars all over every part of your body!
>
> Nicka, 16

Whoa

Before we move on, remember—no matter how low some girls are on the friendship-ability scale, please don't condemn them.

And please don't call them the names we've chosen for the categories on low friend potential, all right? We're using shorthand here to get the point across, but that's no excuse to label any girl ever. It isn't cool to brand anyone with an unflattering name. And just because we don't like a girl's antifriendship acts, it *never* means we don't like her.

> I always give other girls a friendly smile, even the worst chicks in school. Why not? It's free and it makes me feel better. And maybe them too.
>
> Sabina, 18

From this moment on, you're at the cutting edge of friendship. You're a trendsetter, a fun friend getter, a powerful force for the fabulousness of friendship. As such you'll help other girls around the world to be better bud material. Each girl will gain in stature, in strength, in power, in inner beauty, and in feeling much better.

All because of you!

Trouble is a sieve through which we sift our acquaintances.
Those too big to pass through are our friends. Arlene Francis

Chapter 1
The Airhead

n., s.: A spastic, pain-in-the-neck chick, a no-picnic chick. She can also be a neurotic or erratic chick, or a phobic or pathetic chick.

What Makes a Girl an Airhead?

Yikes. You see her being dropped off at school in the morning, pouring out of the car, her books every which way. Her flowery Gap skirt is pinned with a baby-diaper pin. Her eyes have a faraway look. Her striped socks don't match, and the Birkenstocks she has on are way too big.

But maybe that's just today. This is no geek chick really. The next day she comes in wearing a designer career suit and spiky heels. But always on the wrong day or at the wrong place. Career day was last week, but this girl forgot! Or maybe not. Anyway, it seems like she's always late, always vague, and always aiming straight for you—and you have the urge to flat-out run.

But you can't. You let her borrow your chemistry notebook to catch up on her work. But instead of returning it to you all in one piece, she took it apart, lost some pages, and gave you only half of it back, and that's all smudged, splotched, and sticky. Even though you told her to be careful, and even though she promised, promised, *promised,* the notebook is ruined. Now she looks at you and says, "What's wrong with you? Are you having a bad day?" And you feel like screaming, *"What's wrong with* me*? Are you crazy?"*

You have just been nailed by the Airhead.

Dear Dr. Erika:

One of my best friends, Cindi, has never hidden her irresponsibility and forgetfulness. But she's also one of the nicest and most empathetic people you'll ever meet. But this girl would probably miss a lunch date with the Pope if I didn't remind her.

When I received word that I would be traveling to New York for the summer for a dance clinic, my mind raced. I'd get to stay with my aunt, who lives in Manhattan! She said I could bring a friend along with me. Naturally I called Cindi and relayed the good news and we made plans for New York together.

The week before we were to leave was the most hectic in my life. When I called Cindi to see if she was ready to leave for the airport, I was more than shocked to hear she wasn't home.

Thinking that perhaps she'd gone to Wal-Mart for a few last-minute toiletries, I called her cell phone. When an intro of loud music followed by an iffy "Hello?" greeted me, I shouted, "Where are you? The plane leaves in two hours."

Cindi "forgot" that we were supposed to fly to New York! But I could only go if another girl went with me. Since I'm 17, my parents thought as long as my aunt would pick us up at the airport in NYC, we'd be all right. So, of course I couldn't go now. I was devastated. Heartbroken.

Leela, 17

Sounds as if Leela is dealing with an Airhead.

FYI

The Airhead is a girl who's a flake, a ditz, someone permanently in la-la land—in short, a girl who can be totally unreliable and disorganized. She's more absentminded than the proverbial professor. She always forgets to meet you when she promised, is late for the SAT after the hour has been announced a zillion times, loses important info and your best pink cashmere sweater. Seems like she doesn't even remember her middle name, her home phone number, or any deadline, ever.

> I know this one girl who always got her head in the clouds. Whew, she's trouble 'cause you can't count on her. Not ever.
>
> Sierra, 13

Don't write them off right away! These girls are wonderful, bright, successful girls, but for various reasons they're always either a step behind or ahead, or not even anywhere near the path the other girls are on. For example, when there's a time change, the Airhead might miss it and show up an hour late or early, wondering where everyone is. But when the whole school system is closed due to bad weather, she trudges in on time and asks, surprised, "What happened?"

> This girl I know is a total disaster. Everything about her is, like, out of whack. And what's worse, she's always making me late and look bad too.
>
> Asia, 17

Oh, the Airhead—she's perfectly all right, but she's just a little (or a lot!) scatterbrained because she has never learned to take responsibility for her actions or inactions. Since she's cute or funny or has a special talent, people have always overlooked her "weirdness."

> There's this nice girl in my class that's way out of step. Two weeks after a project is due, she calls me and asks, "Now when do we turn in that leaf collection?"
>
> Marie, 14

So even though the Airhead can be nice and cute and often means well, be warned. After that, proceed with caution with her. You don't have to write her off, just watch out!

So why is the Airhead so absentminded?

Freedom High School, USA

By the time Bethany gets to school, she's already been up for hours and done a day's work. Fact is, her mother, Greta, goes to all these dance competitions and wins lots of shiny trophies, so she's not around a lot to take care of things around the house.

Bethany knows not to call Greta "Mom" to her face, only "Greta." Bethany loves her mom and her brothers, but it's hard to keep everything going, including school, with the boys being just nine months old. Bethany is in charge of feeding them and getting them to the sitter. On top of that, she has to pack their diapers and a change of clothes, plus all their food.

Of course, Grandma would take the twins in a sec. And Bethany could probably live there, too. But that lady is tough. Goes by the rules. Bethany would have to make some major changes in her go-with-the-flow lifestyle, but Bethany likes her freedom. Still, she gets real nervous every time Greta says if Bethany complains about the twins one more time, she'll ship them off to their dad. 'Cause Bethany doesn't want that either.

Anyway, by the time she gets to school, she has her mind on a million things, and even before the twins came, there never was a regular schedule at her house. So, Bethany stays up late whenever she wants to, watches whatever on TV. She never gets enough sleep. Eats on the run. Half a cold soy burger for breakfast. Or a handful of nuts. As a result, Bethany finds it hard to get into the school routine.

Bethany is late wandering into first period, and the class is deep into the lesson. The teacher lets Bethany slide, though. Most of the teachers do.

Her friends have been waiting for her. One of them has been taking notes for her, another keeps a special file just for Bethany. In that file she puts all the handouts and other stuff Bethany wouldn't even know about if it wasn't for her caring classmates.

But for some reason, Bethany isn't bothered in the least that other girls have to double up. They moan and roll their eyes, but so what? She feels glad she had friends scurrying around and getting her up to speed. Hey, as long as she is the class Airhead, she's got somebody and isn't alone. Feeling like she's all alone might be scary. So, being the superditz in the crowd is better than nothing. Isn't it? Of course, Bethany could get a clock. She could keep a calendar. She could write down the due dates and reminders. The schedules, the notes in class. And maybe someday she will.

Of course, whatever is going on in the Airhead's life that influences her to be so unfocused, so in a constant fog, is something you should try to understand. It's tough to live in a family that isn't like yours or the other girls'. When a girl grows up without a schedule and no rules, she doesn't learn to plan and stick to it. So, an Airhead's life often isn't easy as pie. Perhaps you can help the Airheads you know now and then. But you can't quickly bring order and structure into a vacuum. You cannot quickly end all the confusion in the Airhead's circumstances. So, the Airhead can and will inconvenience you, but that's nothing dangerous—just something to deal with.

Okay, so the Airhead may have her head waaaay up in the clouds, but she's still a nice girl on the inside. The best thing for you to do is try and be understanding—but don't let her Airhead ways run your life! Take the quiz below to find out if you're on Airhead overload.

FAST FRIENDSHIP FITNESS TEST

Could You Be an Airhead Magnet?

1 The Airhead in your class has chosen you as her best and only friend. You:

a. Feel bad for her and spend lots of time with her, even though she's not really respectful of your time and your stuff. You figure maybe you can help keep her organized, so you're always trying to get her to pay attention and stuff—even though she doesn't seem to notice or appreciate it.

b. Like her "go with the flow" attitude. Until you met her, you would have never imagined leaving the house without your Palm Pilot or showing up even a *second* late for class.

But now that you're hanging with her, the teachers actually let you get away with stuff like that. Cool!

c. Don't have time for her ditzy drama. She always looks so lost! And her clothes never match. The girls in your clique never talk to her, which means that you stay as far away from her as possible.

d. Realize that she's a nice girl—she just can't get it together sometimes. So, you help her whenever you can, but you don't let her Airhead antics rub off on you. After all, you have your own life and your own goals.

2 The teacher assigns the Airhead to your group project. You:

a. Groan inside. You've worked with the Airhead before, and you know that you'll spend most of your time picking up her slack if you want to make the grade. Still, it's easier than counting on her to get her work done on time.

b. Aren't worried about it. You'll just have a private meeting with everyone else in the group to let them know she's a flake. Then you can get organized and get started without her getting in the way.

c. Absolutely refuse to work with her. To get her out of your way, you send her to the library to copy a page from the encyclopedia. As soon as she's gone, you laugh and brush imaginary dandruff off your shirt—like, see how easy it is to get rid of this flake? With the Airhead out of your way, you can make sure the work gets done right—and take the credit for the good grades.

d. Are worried at first, but then you decide to be as helpful as possible. You assign the various parts of the material appropriately and personally help the Airhead get her part done, even if it means having to remind her and working with her slowly. And you know what? Surprise! You're learning lots more yourself by slowing down and showing her what's what. You never knew that teaching could be so empowering!

3 You let the Airhead borrow your fave sweater and she lost it after promising to take good care of it. You:

a. Tell her it's okay, but inside you're really upset. Rather than confront her about it, you decide to blow her off from now on—it's easier than trying to get her to listen to you.

b. Forgive her to her face but tell everyone you know what a loser she is. That was your favorite sweater and you'll never be able to replace it. She's so spacey, she'll never even notice that you're totally talking about her.

c. Are soooo mad at her! You tell her off to her face and you make *sure* everyone hears you do it. So what if you made her cry? She deserved it.

d. Are totally ticked at her. But she's your friend, and you know that even though she's a little ditzy, she means well. You tell her how you feel and let her know that even though you like her, you can't keep letting her borrow your stuff if she's going to lose it or break it.

4 You sit next to the Airhead in study hall. She asks to borrow your Algebra homework overnight, since it's her worst subject. You know that you'll either never see it again, or it will come back stained, ripped, and ruined. You:

a. Make up an excuse to get out of letting her take it. You only lend your homework to your *friends*—not ditzes like her!

b. Give her the homework even though you know you shouldn't. She tries really hard in class, but she's no math genius and if you don't help her out, you worry she'll fail.

c. Say "of course!" in your sweetest voice. Then you give her last week's homework. She's such a dip, she'll never even notice. Maybe *that* will teach her to pay attention!

d. Offer to tutor her during study hall or after school—but tell her that you never let anyone copy your homework.

Now it's time to find out your true FQ: Tally your answers. How many A's, B's, C's, and D's do you have?

3 or 4 A's, check out Answer 1.
3 or 4 B's, check out Answer 2.
3 or 4 C's, check out Answer 3.
3 or 4 D's, check out Answer 4.

If you have a mixture of A's, B's, C's, and D's, look at all the answers. Obviously, there's a bit of everything in you, which is fab. Now can you work on having a little less of the Answer 1 attitude and a little more of the Answer 4 attitude?

Answers

1 Flake Finder

Because of your "so nice" nature, you often let the Airhead get away with things that you shouldn't. It's okay to help the Airhead from time to time, but letting her lazy ways affect your life is no way to shine. So, lend a helping hand when you can, but know when enough is enough.

2 Busybody

Hey there, teenage drama queen! You just love, love, love it when some girl is getting in trouble. Gives you time to shine, right? The more other girls are disorganized and scatterbrained, the better it makes you look. But watch out—the Airhead may *seem* out of it, but she notices a lot more than you think. So, instead of spreading gossip, why not try spreading some good stuff every once in a while?

3 Antifriend

Wow, you're a take-no-prisoners, take-charge kind of girl! Natch, you have no patience for slackers, sluggards, laggards, or dreamers. You're going on with the action, even if you have to create it yourself. For sure, your drive will take you far. Just remember, Ms. Get Out of My Way, that it can be lonely at the top. If you don't stop to lend a helping hand now and then, who is going to be around to help you when you need it?

4 Goal Getter

You're not only a go-getter but also a goal getter. And one goal you have is to help other girls along in their personal quest for success. That's because you have a big heart and reach your hand out to those girls around you who need help. So, don't change a thing! Stay true to yourself and those around you and you're sure to go far!

AIRHEAD FACTORS

What Should You Know about the Airhead?

☑ Know this: An Airhead may be very sweet overall and have a good heart, but she is way scatterbrained and rattled. Everyone has a bad day now and then, but the Airhead has them *all* the time! Nonstop. Every day. No matter what, she always seems to be a few steps behind.

One of my friends never remembers anything I tell her. That's sooo frustrating—it's like she does it on purpose. Like she wants to drive me crazy.

Jordan, 14

☑ The Airhead truly doesn't mean to make you go crazy, but you get that feeling sometimes and who can blame you? It can be maddening to watch her listen to you, nod her head, and tell you she will hold up her end of the bargain. But she never does!

☑ Frequently, that means more than 75 percent of the time, the Airhead simply forgets what she's supposed to do. Or when. Or how. Or she loses the phone number, misplaces the assignment sheet, or gets caught up in something else. And she's in a fog about even routine everyday stuff.

So, if you feel like it and have the time—and it may take a whole whopping lot—you can help the Airhead out by teaching her some basics, like how to plan, how to be on time, how to write down one's deadlines. How can you do this? Check out the next section for some easy tips.

FIRST AID
What You Should Do about the Airhead

There are any number of things you can do for the sake of this flake. Most importantly, you want her to get a grip on her own issues so you don't get stuck carrying her load!

What you want is for her to become more responsible, but you want to do this without becoming her mother!

So here are three things to try:

1. *Even though she's your friend, you have to stand up for yourself.* Don't let her monopolize you all the time and slow down your progress. And never let her ditzy ways take away the time/energy you need to live your own life.
2. *The Airhead is so much easier to deal with in a group.* So, involve others in the flake remake. In a nice and friendly way, enlist the help of other girls and together work on letting the air out of the Airhead—by pulling together, you can help the Airhead pull together!
3. *Take it slow with the Airhead.* Step by step, help her in small things first, then in larger ones. Lend a hand and make sure she can always turn to you—in a real emergency. But don't put your own life on hold. Don't refuse to go out for a sport or join a club just 'cause the Airhead doesn't want to or isn't up for it. You march on.

Never allow the biggest Airhead in your crowd to distract you from your big plan. Otherwise it's her gain but YOUR pain!

Ellie, 16

FIRST PERSON

How I Handled It–Nicole's Real-Life Story

Dumb, dumb. That's what I am, really. Just dumb.

I was totally thrilled when my drama teacher put me in charge of our school's fall play, *Our Town.* It was a blast, being in charge at last. I was really blissed out. It was the first time that the teacher turned everything over to me—yay! It was my first chance to show off my talents—after all, I plan to major in Theater in college. And there I was, in just eleventh grade and running the whole show.

I went to town on *Our Town.* I handed out assignments—everything from the set, the lighting, the props, the understudies, the music, the sound system. *Everything.* And I didn't get stressed out!

The kids in Drama Club are supertalented students, so it was no prob getting everyone assigned something fab. Except for this one girl, Julie, who is sooo spacey. But I really wanted to be fair. Everyone makes fun of her and stuff because she's a space cadet, but I wanted to give her a chance. She's really sweet! So, I gave Julie the programs to do. The programs! Hello? That's only one of the most important jobs, so I was glad to give it to her. But on dress-rehearsal day, there were no programs. Julie came late and handed out zilch. So everyone thought maybe she was saving the programs for the Saturday show. The opening. Well, she did.

But every name was misspelled, and my name was left out totally. What an embarrassment. Now I have nothing to put into my portfolio where I keep all the programs of shows I've ever been a part of. I was so upset that I got in a big screaming fight with Julie and I made her cry. Worse, everybody in the whole school hates, *hates* me for being so dumb.—Nicole, 16

CHICK-POINT

Grade the Girls

F *

D **

C ***

B ****

A *****

Chick Grades: **

Two stars for both of you, Julie and Nicole. Julie—you should have paid closer attention to detail. After all, Nicole was trying to give you a chance. And Nicole—not having one's name spelled right in a high school production is awful, but it isn't like cold-blooded murder, so you shouldn't carry on so.

Plus—how could you give the *one* job that demands serious attention to details to a girl known for being spacey? To a girl who didn't have her act together the night before? Who had nothing at all to hand out, not even a rough draft of the program?

You should have demanded to see a copy of the program a week before, or earlier. That way, you could have proofed it yourself and an artist could've done the layout. For your supervision of Julie, you get two stars. For your great work on the play, though, you get five!

Dear Diary

Okay, it's journal time! This section will help you make a friend journal that will help you discover lots of cool things about yourself—and your friends. Grab a notebook or some loose-leaf paper and a folder. Decorate it any way you wish.

Defining Moments

Okay, now you've got your journal just the way you want it. On the first page, write down this question: *What is a friend?*

Now, write your answer underneath. Remember, there are no rights and wrongs here. This is your own special definition. What is your definition of a friend?

> To me a friend is someone nice who's always there for me. Also a friendly person whom I can talk to whenever, and who helps me.
>
> Erin-Hsu, 16

List Lesson

Okay, you've got your friend definition written down, right? Next, list the names of your friends on the paper. Don't worry about how many names are on your list! Everyone's number will be different. Some girls are outgoing and have tons of friends, and some girls prefer having only one or two close friends to share their secrets with.

On the back of the page, list some of the girls from your school who perhaps you'd like to be friends with. Then write down what's kept you from becoming friends with them—so far. What's been the obstacle?

Keep It Simple!

Okay, these exercises may seem really simple—and they are. But with each chapter, you'll fill in a little more.

Before you close the folder for today, look back at your definition of a friend. You'll probably find words such as *nice* and *friendly* in combination with *is always there for me and helps me,* et cetera. Then think of the Airhead in your group. Though she may be nice and friendly, she has a weakness or two. She isn't known for her dependability or her follow-through. That means, she doesn't possess *all* the top friend traits, but she's got some of them. So, it's up to you to focus on those good-friend qualities she has and help her develop more. In the process you'll become a better friend yourself.

FRIEND SPOTTING

The Airhead

So, now you know what makes the Airhead tick. You know that she means well, even if her head is in the clouds. And you know that you can help her without letting her drag you down. But how can you be sure you've encountered the Airhead? Watch out for any girl who:

- ☑ Is always late for school, classes, and meetings.
- ☑ Repeats the same mistakes every day, week, or month. For example—she's always running to the nurse's office for supplies because her period just started and she's not prepared.
- ☑ Always calls you in a panic. For example, she calls you on Sunday night after midnight (your mom is going to kill you!),

waking you from a sound sleep and asking, "When's that descriptive essay due? Monday or Tuesday?"

Stay clear of any girl who needs more than three chances to fly right. But never, ever does. If you hang with her, you'll regret it.

Leigh, 17

Great point, Leigh.

Rx for Airheadaches

So remember—appreciate the Airhead and enjoy the time you spend with her, but don't let her ditzy ways drag *you* down. Stay open to meeting new girls. Even the new friends you'll meet may have a ditz in their ranks, but just think of all the friendship potential out there. As long as you know not to count on the Airhead 100 percent and to just appreciate her for what she is, for what she *can* offer, you'll do great. There are hundreds of other girls in your school, in your world, just waiting to be friends with you.

All you need to do is take heart and make a start. Here's a fast friendship rule: With any girl you meet, be nice, be friendly, and be yourself.

You can always start a conversation with the girl next to you in line or wherever. Even a girl you've never met before. You never know what they have to say and this could be your best friend in hiding!

Kelsey, 16

Chicks Mix

As you open your eyes wide to all the other girls your age who also want to make new friends, great friends—just like you—keep thinking of the huge friendship pool that's all around you. And this pool is constantly growing. Yes, new girls are moving to your school district this moment. New faces appear on the tennis team, in the cafeteria, and in the Honor Club.

Class Actions

Be bold and mix it up with the new girls any chance you get. Take a deep breath and step out of your comfort zone by saying hi to any new girls that you run across. And when other girls turn away from the new Airhead entering your school or class, don't. No way, you're not going to snub or snob her. You know that you're able to protect yourself from any negative, or not-so-hot, tendencies she might have. So take the first step, smile, and say hello.

Chick-Mate

In every group of girls there is always one who—for some reason or other—has her head constantly in the clouds. She's very forgetful, unreliable, and absentminded. She's the Airhead, whom many other girls shy away from—but you don't. That's a great attitude to have and you're to be commended.

1. So be her friend if she's willing to come through for you. That means, if the Airhead is showing signs of becoming more reliable, encourage her. If she's willing to pick up on pointers and she tries to do better—and if she apologizes when she messes up, whereas before she never did!—then keep encouraging her and being her friend. You go, girl. And should she slide back into her Airheadedness once or twice, laugh it off. We all make mistakes.
2. But if she *never* changes and doesn't act like she really cares, then don't let your pet project girl take you away from the many other girls whose friendship potential is way higher. Sure, anytime you have extra energy to spare, help the Airhead find herself, help her with school, and help her with her problems. And guide or direct her to others who can help her out even more. But don't ever get caught in a car with her doing the driving! Or spend all your free time with her.

3. If you don't keep yourself open to meeting new friends, you're missing out on some really great chicks who are just waiting for you to discover them as your fab friends and best buds.

They want to be in your group, in your circle. Please let them.

FRIENDSHIP RATING SCALE

The Friendship Rating Scale goes from 1 to 10 (with 1 being way low and 10 being tops), which will help you make up your mind about which girls are hot friendship-wise and which for sure are not. You'll see a Friendship Rating at the end of each chapter!

Friendship Finder

On the Friendship Rating Scale, the Airhead is a 3, 4, 5, or maybe even a 6.

1	Kick yourself for ever thinking about trying to be friends with her.
2	Serious waste of time.
3	May be a waste of time.
4	One more try can't hurt.
5	If you feel like investing more time, that's fine.
6	Keep trying to be her friend.
7	Try harder.
8	Try harder and smarter.
9	Put making friends with this girl on the top of your list.
10	Really strive to be friends with her. Then you will thrive.

Friend Lines: It's the friends you can call at 4:00 a.m. that matter. Marlene Dietrich

Chapter 2
The Me-Me Chick

n., s.: A selfish or egotistic chick, a plastic chick, a cliquey chick. She may seem like lots of fun—but look a little deeper to see if there's more to her than "me."

What Makes a Girl a Me-Me Chick?

She can hardly wait to get to school because she has loads to dish. As soon as she swishes through the door, you see her take her place in the middle of her group, gabbing away with gusto, and with all her followers listening, nodding, and taking it all in. Whatever she's going on about. Which is tons.

And that's always the latest awesome buzz—all about herself and what she's thinking about at the moment. Like the latest Britney wedding. And how long she personally thinks this one will last. Or who she thinks the hottest Hollywood hunk is, was, will be. Or who she has decided will win the Oscars this year, or not. But it's always all about her ideas, her thoughts. Her take on stuff. It's always her in the spotlight.

If, however, you offer your input or ask her about something other than herself and her world, for example, the emergency student government meeting that's been called to discuss the homecoming parade, she shrugs and says, "Who cares? Why should I? Duh. I'm riding on that float, not making it."

Then she dishes all about the new dress she'll be wearing. It's in her colors and her style and she picked it out. It's going to be so much fabber than those of the other attendants. She gestures passionately as she describes her glam gown and tells a funny story about the size of the girls riding the old agriculture float. Soon everyone's laughing and crowding around her even more, even though they've already heard this story before. Three times.

But this is typical for the Me-Me Chick.

Dear Dr. Erika:
This girl has been my friend ever since fourth grade. We've been in classes together ever since and have been through so much and we could always talk about everything and laugh about stuff, you know? Not anymore. When I tell her about a problem now, she looks at me like I'm speaking Urdu. Then before you know it, she's back to talking about *her* issues. Like about her room that she wants to redo, or her nails, or whatever. Here I'm trying to tell her about serious stuff like worries, you know?

But the moment I open my mouth, my friend cuts me off. She tells me how much better she thinks she'd look if she'd only let her hair grow like Jennifer Aniston's. By that time lunch is over and I haven't had a chance to get in more than three words.

Pamela, 15

FYI

The Me-Me Chick is a girl whose whole world revolves around just one thing—her. Her opinions, feelings, ideas, fashion sense, latest news. She spends hours discussing every single detail of her life—like the shade of nail polish she's considering for her next pedicure—should she go with Cherry Red, Raspberry Red, Ruby Red, Ripple Red, Really Red, Rose Red, Rad Red, or Red-Purple?

She always has an audience, and she always makes sure they're paying close attention to her. When she senses that her audience is growing bored, she usually injects some drama into her story to put herself back in the spotlight. She spilled soda on her brand-new Seven jeans. Or her shoes are giving her blisters, or whatever! All she ever talks about are her life and her future. Her, her, her.

She never brings up an issue that would require asking anyone else for *her* opinion. That would be open to discussion. No, she's made up her mind and that's it. Even if something should come up—something that matters beyond the moment, something controversial, something like real life—she's very skillful at directing the topic back to her.

Wow, the Me-Me Chick is quick. The moment you say, "Well, what I think is—" she makes a smooth transition to something that happened to her this morning on the way to school. Should you ever force her flat-out to listen to anything you have to say, she goes, "Yeah, right, sure, uh-huh." Impatiently, with her foot tapping. But whatever you tell her, it's always in one ear and out the other. Fast. Then she's off again full-steam and gushing about what she really, really wants for her big birthday. Are you guys taking notes?

On the surface, the Me-Me Chick seems like a fun friend. But once you get to know her, you begin to get the feeling that this girl doesn't care about anyone besides herself. And she really doesn't want to hear about your thoughts or your opinions.

So all that preoccupation with herself and with surface stuff—to the exclusion of caring for anyone else's thoughts or more serious issues—makes her friendship potential not hot.

> This girl I know talks about herself, like, 99 percent of the time; the rest of the time it's all about her family.
>
> Shelby, 14

Fact is, when you're around the Me-Me Chick, nothing matters but her me-me-dom.

> One of my best friends, she, like, sees everything, like, in relation to her. Her hair, her horse, her house. It's never what I say, nor even hearsay. It's all her-say.
>
> Leigh, 15

Freedom High School, USA

Kylie doesn't want to miss school ever—it's way too much fun. Life is waaaay too much fun. At home, she gets everything she wants. At school, she gets everything she wants. Her life is totally set. Her parents are so worried, they let her get away with everything. Yet, they treat her like she's the most precious and most fragile Fabergé egg in the world. It all started with Kylie's older brother. When he was a college freshman, he got some rare disease. And he died. Ever since then, everyone's worried about Kylie all the time, even though the doctors said it was a fluke. One in a zillion. And now they even have a treatment for the disease! But still, every time she sneezes, her parents have her in the emergency room. But she enjoys all the attention she's getting. And she's learned to expect it from her parents, friends, and teachers. At first, it was scary, but now Kylie loves it. After all, her friends couldn't do without her and all her exciting news. So, now she tries to make every day exciting.

Before school, Kylie skillfully applies the hottest new shade of eggplant eye shadow and puts on her newest outfit. The pleated skirt is too short for her school's dress code, and the matching top exposes her tan midriff, another no-no. But with a shirt over it, she'll get by. And even if she's sent to the principal's office, Mom doesn't care. She'll just whip over to school and sign her out, and then the two of them will enjoy brunch at the club and still have time to shop at Saks.

Mom gave Kylie a cell phone for just this reason, so Kylie can call her whenever a teacher starts picking on her. Which they better not—especially not after what Kylie and her family have been through. And *extra* especially not over something as silly as the dumb dress code. Kylie knows what's in style and she's teaching all her many friends. She's like a walking fountain of fashion info. So, why doesn't the school finally get out of the Dark Ages?

As Kylie prances into the lobby of the enormous main school building, she's mobbed by her friends, who tell her how glad they are to see her. Today's news: Kylie's mom is going to take her shopping in London this summer!

Everyone knows that Kylie's mom is so great. Because Mom's always so worried about Kylie, she rearranged her whole life to be flexible. She does her real estate work only when Kylie's in school, and she gives Kylie whatever she wants. If it weren't for her, Kylie wouldn't have her own credit card and her new Mercedes E something or other. And a subscription to every hot magazine.

As Kylie is filling in her friends about what her plans are for her big trip, Courtney enters the lobby, hobbling on crutches, her foot in a cast. All of the girls gasp and begin chattering as Courtney joins them. Courtney is the best soccer player in school. She broke her ankle during the conference match the day before but not until after she had scored the winning goal.

As Kylie's friends gush over Courtney, Kylie takes a deep breath and goes, *"Cat-choo, cat-choo. Cat-choo,"* while holding her chest. That makes her crew focus on her again, fast, and ask, "Are you all right?" It's a trick that she uses with her mom, too.

Once the attention is back on Kylie, she resumes telling everyone about her trip . . . her passport . . . her luggage . . . her shopping spree at Harrods . . .

> Every morning before school, we meet in the lobby and everyone in my group is excited 'cause they have lots on their mind. But there's this one girl who never lets anyone else talk. She, like, monopolizes every single conversation.
>
> Dallas, 14

But what's going on underneath? Do you think that Kylie is really happy playing her charades all day, every day? No way! Underneath all the Me-Me mania, she's a smart, beautiful girl just waiting to emerge, even if she drives you crazy! But just because she's stuck in "me" mode doesn't mean you have to suffer. Or does it?

Check out the quiz below to find out if you're holding your own against the Me-Me Chick . . . or if you're just one of her crowd.

FAST FRIENDSHIP FITNESS TEST

Could You Be a Me-Me Chick Magnet?

1 The Me-Me Chick in your class has decided to include you in her inner circle. You:

a. Are so pleased to have been chosen! This is the best thing that's ever happened to you in your whole life. The Me-Me Chick is always getting tons of attention, and if you're in her group, maybe you'll get attention, too. After all, you're sick of fading into the background all the time.

b. Become her most faithful follower and offer to fetch and carry for her—whatever she wants. You follow her around like a faithful pup, listening to all of her stories and advising her through all of her daily crises.

c. Refuse to share the spotlight with her. Why should this girl get all the attention all the time? Just to outdo her, you form your own group, and you make sure they all pay attention to *you*. You'll outtalk, outplay, and outdo her if it's the last thing you do!

d. Don't feel the need to be "accepted" into her group. You've got lots of friends. Instead, you accept her as she is, a fun but egotistic chick that can make you laugh. Sure, you appreciate her fashion sense and ask her what the hot colors are—or not. But you seek good friends who believe in the give-and-take of relationships elsewhere. So there.

2 The Me-Me Chick has been placed into your group and has elected herself leader. Your assignment is to make flash cards for the SAT vocabulary section. The Me-Me Chick decides that your group should make fashion flashcards instead. And instead of writing SAT-word sentences, she decrees that quotes on styles are needed. She hands out twenty-five cards to each of you and asks you to interview her for a hot tip. You:

a. Would rather study for the SAT, since fashion isn't your thing. But it's easier to follow her lead than deal with the consequences, so you grudgingly oblige.

b. Scurry to the library and rifle through *YM, Seventeen,* and *Teen Vogue* to find the top tips, then get her take on them so you can quote her. Ooh, you're so excited to help her!

c. Think, *who is this girl to tell me what to do?* Her self-involvement means diddly-squat to you. You take the notecards and write mean messages to her on each one, then you pass them out to the group. No girly-girl is going to boss you around!

d. Think it's silly at first, but then you have an idea—combining boring SAT words with the latest fads. You share your idea with the Me-Me Chick and the group. Instant success! It turns out to be a fun way to make the words interesting and stick in your memory. "The use of citrus colors on handbags and shoes was most *efficacious.*" Wow.

3 You've decided to run for class president. The Me-Me Chick immediately volunteers to be your campaign manager. You:

a. Really wanted to do this on your own, but you're afraid to say no to her. So, you agree to let her run your campaign.

b. Tell her that she's so much better suited to run for president, and you offer to help *her* run instead. After all, you're no match for her. You launch into preparations and don't make another move without getting her approval.

c. Tell her that you don't want her anywhere near your campaign. Got that?! And if she keeps coming anywhere near you during the next few weeks, you'll report her to the FBI for stalking.

d. Thank her for her offer and tell her you have a better job for her in mind. The candidates always give a speech to the student body before the election. Part of that speech is a skit. Since she's great in front of a crowd, maybe she can be in charge of the skit instead?

4 The Me-Me Chick has been selected to give the speech at the upcoming school assembly. You:

a. Are sooo glad she was picked and not you. It's scary to speak in front of a whole lot of people and there's nothing you have to say that would interest anyone, anyway. You probably would have messed it up.

b. Tell her you're glad she's been chosen. You can't wait to sit in the front row and clap for her so everyone will see that she's your friend. You can't wait to hear whatever she has to say, even if she just repeats *Manolo Blahnik* fifty times.

c. Launch a plan of attack. You mobilize a ton of friends to heckle her during her speech—see if she likes being the center of attention when everyone is laughing at her!

d. Congratulate her on getting chosen—she's great in front of a crowd and you're sure she'll represent the class well. There are plenty more speeches coming up, and you know that you'll get your shot someday soon.

Now it's time to find out your FQ: Tally your answers. How many A's, B's, C's, and D's do you have?

3 or 4 A's check out Answer 1.
3 or 4 B's check out Answer 2.
3 or 4 C's check out Answer 3.
3 or 4 D's check out Answer 4.

If you have a mixture of A's, B's, C's, and D's, look at all the answers. Obviously, there's a bit of everything in you, which is fab. Now, can you work on having a little less of the Answer 1 attitude and a little more of the Answer 4 attitude?

Answers

Enabling Erica

By never speaking up to the Me-Me Chick, you're making your own life harder. How will she ever change her ways if you don't tell her what's what? We don't live under a monarchy, so why do you let her rule your life? Next time she asks you to do something you don't like, try telling her about it! You might feel a lot better.

Toady Jody

You act like you were born to spit-polish her boots, then lie down and let her walk all over you. You're so starstruck that you can't make a move without Ms. Me-Me giving a nod. Why? If you spend all of your time following someone else's lead, how are you ever going to discover the fabulous girl who's inside of you?

Uncool Julie

You get too hot under the collar too quick any time you don't get all the attention or feel deprived or put upon. Take a deep breath—life isn't a competition. Why are you so focused on what the Me-Me Chick is doing, anyway? Are you a Me-Me Chick in disguise? Think about it!

Pal Perfect

Good for you! You think before you act. Plus, you keep an open mind about the girls in your world. What makes a group of friends fantastic is that different kinds of girls are part of it, and you're a friend to anyone who does their fair share. You know better than to be a personal assistant, and you're not a power maniac, either. You always do your best to be a good pal—keep up the good work!

ME-ME CHICK FACTORS

What Should You Know about the Me-Me Chick?

A Me-Me Chick doesn't create herself. Most often she's a girl who has been babied from birth on or shortly thereafter. You've heard about spoiled brats, well, this girl is a spoiled rotten brat, most likely. Often her whole family just orbits around her. Plus, she's been sheltered or overprotected. So, nothing disagreeable has ever been allowed to cross her path, or if it did, not for long. Her parents have built a thick protective wall around her and let nothing even slightly "heavy" come near her. So, how can you get smart about the Me-Me Chick? Read on:

- ☑ By now, the Me-Me Chick has gotten so used to being the center of everyone's attention that she's learned to expect, demand, and command it. And along with her ever-growing need to be a star, her methods of obtaining the huge amount of attention she requires have expanded. Her methods can include acting like a baby, being dramatic, shedding crocodile tears, and developing other attention-seeking mannerisms.
- ☑ The Me-Me Chick's behavior is often encouraged by her family, like you learned from Kylie's story. The whole clan, and especially her mother, grandmother, aunts, and cousins think she's just *so* adorable. On top of that, they might even hope that she'll fulfill their childhood wishes that never came true—like becoming prom queen or class president or whatever. That's a lot of pressure for a young girl!
- ☑ Look for the good! No matter what you see on the outside, every girl has good stuff on the inside. The Me-Me Chick is trying to figure out her way in the world, just like everyone else.

FIRST AID

What You Should Do about the Me-Me Chick

1. Realize that this chick is the product of her upbringing. She's been trained to think of herself first, second, third, and so on. She thrives on the limelight. Recognize that you can't change her—you can only change yourself. If you don't like what she's doing, let her know about it in a polite way.

   One friend I have does nothing but chitchat about herself and her issues. And when the rest of us chime in, she pouts.

   Hope, 15

2. Old habits may be hard to break for this type of girl, but if you really like her, talk with her. Get to know her better; get some insight into her background. Once you get to know her, maybe you can figure out a way to tell her that the girl world is not a monarchy with her as the queen.

   Friendship is a two-way street, not a one-way alley with you always giving, giving, giving and the other girl always taking, taking, taking.

   Tania, 17

3. If you know the Me-Me Chick well enough, ask her if she minds if you do an experiment. From now on, you'll count every statement she makes about herself and compare it to the number of those she lets other girls make. Can she see the difference in the numbers?

   There's this one girl in my crowd who's always going on about her stuff. So, one day at lunch I timed her. She went on for twenty-five minutes. Problem was, lunch was only twenty minutes. She was still at it five minutes into class—and all about nothing but her.

   Elisa, 16

FIRST PERSON

How I Handled It–Jennie's Real-Life Story

I'm the kind of girl who works her heart out. I really, really do. I think doing your best at all times is what I should do. Anyway, I try. So, when our Drama Club was planning its fall production, my friends and I decided to sign up for the production end, which nobody liked that much. Still, we had a blast. We went wild painting the backdrops and got real creative rounding up the lavish furniture that we had to beg, borrow, or even "steal for a short time" from our families. Me and my guys did a bang-up job. They even voted me assistant production director and did I feel proud. I felt like I had finally "arrived." I mean, it was hard work but it paid off.

Then came the fun part. After the props were ready, I invited my whole crew to my house for homemade pizza. I spent my own hard-earned cash on the ingredients, then polled the gang to find out what they liked best—vegetarian, sausage, pepperoni, or chicken? A few of my friends came over early, and we shopped for hours at a fancy-food place and chopped for eons. Finally, we got the pizzas baked. That meant we had to get permission to borrow my neighbor's double oven too.

Then the star, Meredith, arrived with her entourage. She's so into herself! She played the lead, and the newspaper had just done a story on her. She came in with her group and looked at everything we made very carefully, like it was some kind of test. Some of the girls started oohing and aahing over the food and the decorations and the way we had fixed everything up. They asked me for advice on how to plan some cool event at their houses. All the girls clustered around my helpers and me and complimented us. And for a minute, it felt really great.

That's when Meredith started whining about how her day was so rough and how she was so sad that she messed up her lines and how everything in the play was just all wrong. And can you guess what happened next? She said she didn't actually feel like eating pizza after all! It was she who had insisted on pizza in the first place! Then Meredith just stood there and talked about her fear factor of carb overload. And how her capris wouldn't snap anymore, and how bad she'd look in the morning with her tummy pouching out. And she went on and on. In the meantime, the pizzas got cold; the ice melted in the tea. The sodas got flatter than a pancake. Then Queen Meredith claimed she wanted to go out for salads instead. I offered to make her a salad, but she wrinkled up her nose and said she had a stomachache. Then she said she shouldn't eat at all, and she only came over because she felt bad that we worked so hard on the pizza. In the end, she left with her crew, and a lot of other girls left with her.

So, I wrapped the pizzas in foil, stuck them in the freezer. Next time all I'll have to do is pull them out and nuke them.—Jennie, 16

Chick Grades: *****

A triple chick-minus for Meredith who developed a very convenient stomachache. She ought to save her acting for Broadway.

And five stars for you, Jennie, and your helpers for working so hard to get the cool refreshments ready. You went to a lot of trouble and expense. And also to the other girls who complimented you and asked for your hot advice—they did great too.

> CHICK-POINT
> **Grade the Girls**
> F *
> D **
> C ***
> B ****
> A *****

But listen up: Those five stars are only temporary. If you and the other girls let the same fiasco happen to all of you the next time around, you will lose them. What all of you should have done is have someone help Meredith get home safely. In the meantime, the rest of you should have feasted on the perfect pizzas, played your fave CDs, discussed whatever, and had a ball.

Dear Diary

Okay, if you've always wanted to tell the Me-Me Chick how you feel, now's your chance. Get your diary out and get ready to write. Write a letter to the Me-Me Chick in your life and tell her how you feel. You never even have to give her the letter at all. What's important is that you pour out whatever's on your mind and tell her how her "me mania" makes you feel. Don't hold back! This is your chance to get your feelings out.

Learning Lists

After you've finished your letter, make a list of all the girls you know who aren't selfish nonstop. The girls who listen to each other—no matter if it's a good day or a bad day. The girls you know you can count on if you need to.

Now think about your own actions. Are you a good friend to those around you? Do you stay away from Me-Me mania, or do you subject your friends to it?

If you can't think of many names—don't worry! Write down a couple of question marks as well. The question marks stand for the names of the girls you will soon meet. They will turn out to be the kind of friends that you can turn to when you need them. And they will turn to you when they need you. And will never turn their backs on you.

> I welcome the chance to be there for my friends 'cause I know they'll be there for me when I need them.
>
> Alise, 14

FRIEND SPOTTING

The Me-Me Chick

You can't change a Me-Me Chick easily. It can be a long process to change any self-centered chick into a giving girl. Therefore, don't let her rule your world.

> If you hang with way selfish girls all the time, you end up way selfish too. I've seen it happen more than once.
>
> Imani, 13

Remember: Being selfish and uncaring is always negative, and you definitely don't want that trait cropping up in yourself, nor do you want to be the victim of it. For that reason, learn to spot the Me-Me Chicks in your crowd so you can avoid them. So, where do they usually hang out?

You'll find them:

- ☑ In the middle of a group of girls talking. They're hardly ever alone.
- ☑ On their cell phone or text messaging. But here's the key—it's always in such a way that it interrupts everyone else. It's never just a quick, quiet phone chat when you're all sitting together at lunch. No, the Me-Me Chick talks and laughs loudly, interrupting someone else no matter where she is—in the middle

of a restaurant, during dinner, the movies, the class play. She simply doesn't care about others.

☑ Bringing their mom and dad to school a lot. Me-Me Chicks are often too into themselves to take any deadlines seriously. They're for everybody else but not for Ms. Me-Me. So, she's appalled when she doesn't get a good grade when she turns in work late. She believes that she can always sigh and cry and no teacher will dare deny her an extension on any project. When that's not happening, in come her folks to protest.

Rx for Minimizing a Me-Metude

It's only natural to have a me-metude once in a while. We all want to be pampered and looked after sometimes. We love being babied now and then. And often we feel we don't get the attention we need, we deserve. But don't ever let your me-metude flat-out rule you. Trim it down to size and minimize it. How?

1. Catch yourself when you find yourself hogging the conversation. Let other girls participate and listen to them. You can learn a lot from them. In general, think of including other girls rather than excluding them.
2. One way to be less of a talk show-off is to ask other girls some questions. Then give them enough time to answer. Sometimes a follow-up question is called for.
3. Think of a talk with your friends as like a tennis game. It's a back-and-forth, with the ball being words. It's not a war where you spar, but a fun exchange of news and views. What you want to show your friends is that you care about them as much as they care about you.

Any girl I see is a friend possibility for me. After a few words I can tell right away if she's a give-and-take girl or just too into herself.

Carter, 14

So just look around. Super good friend material without a me-me streak is all over the place. Wherever you look, you see them in the lobby at school first thing in the morning before class starts. You find them standing by their lockers or in the cafeteria lining up to get their plate of "mystery meat" or after school as they wait for soccer practice to start. If you exude a you-tude and not a me-metude, they'll be drawn to you in no time.

Chicks Mix

One good way to dilute the negative friendship potential of the Me-Me Chicks at your school is to up your own unselfishness. That means, get busy and look beyond your daily group. Make an effort to talk to some girls who aren't a part of your usual group. There are tons of friend possibilities all around you—you just have to open up to meeting them!

Class Actions

Do this little exercise tomorrow at school: Make an effort to talk to a girl in one of your classes whom you don't normally talk to. By reaching out to others, you're making the girl world so much bigger and you're helping to change the negative into positive, right? It's easy to get so wrapped up in your everyday life that you forget to take a look around and see the possibilities. So, take a chance, reach out, and mix it up, girl!

> One of my very best friends is a girl who has a hearing problem. She had an ear infection that caused it. Anyway, sometimes I have to write stuff down for her, or make sure I face her, so she can lip-read. But wow, how her heart can hear. Way better than any other girl I know.
>
> Taylor, 14

Chick-Mate

In a nutshell, there's a Me-Me Chick (or two) in every group of girls. You can't avoid her. She can mean lots of laughs and keep you tickled. But she's low in real friend potential because, as we said, the Me-Me Chick already has her very best and longtime friend: herself!

- Learn a few Me-Me Chick stoppers and use them to help stop the Me-Me Chick in her tracks. So, the next time the Me-Me Chick is pulling her selfish stunts, you can say something like, "Great story—wow." Then turn to the shyest girl in her group and ask her what she thinks. This is a great way to take the attention away from the Me-Me Chick and put it on another girl.
- And what if you're the shyest girl in your group? Why not speak up every once in a while? Let the Me-Me Chick know that you have opinions, too. You'll feel so much better once you do, and you'll also stop the Me-Me Chick in her tracks.
- If you're feeling left out by the Me-Me Chick, seek real friends elsewhere, and you'll be fine. So, accept her for what she is—good for a laugh, good for a giggle, but not good for a true-blue girlfriend.
- Remember that you're the friend expert, or soon will be. So, pass on the info about the Me-Me Chicks and their tricks and have another friend in on your game plan; that is, to include all the girls in the group in the chat.

One way to really make headway with a Me-Me Chick is to get her alone. That's when she may be more open to listen as you, ever so gently, tell her what's so cool about her. And how it would be absolutely fab if she could tone it down—her mighty me-emphasis. Just a tad. Help her to baby-step it down.

FRIENDSHIP RATING SCALE

The Friendship Rating Scale goes from 1 to 10 (with 1 being way low and 10 being tops), which will help you make up your mind about which girls are hot friendship-wise and which for sure are not. You'll see a Friendship Rating at the end of each chapter!

Friendship Finder

Overall, the Me-Me Chick is a 3, 4, 5, or 6 on the Friendship Rating Scale.

1	Kick yourself for ever thinking about trying to be friends with her.
2	Serious waste of time.
3	May be a waste of time.
4	One more try can't hurt.
5	If you feel like investing more time, that's fine.
6	Keep trying to be her friend.
7	Try harder.
8	Try harder and smarter.
9	Put making friends with this girl on the top of your list.
10	Really strive to be friends with her. Then you will thrive.

Lots of people want to ride with you in the limo, but what you want is someone who will take the bus with you when the limo breaks down. Oprah Winfrey

Chapter 3
The Phony

n., s.: A fakey chick, a fair-weather friend only, a hypocritical way-slick chick and lay-it-on-thick chick, a lickety-split-disappearing-act chick

What Makes a Girl a Phony?

Monday morning. Grayson rushes up to you in the library and tells you how totally thrilled she is to see you. The library is where you and your friends hang out before the first bell. You are allowed to whisper, so no prob. But Grayson raises her voice in all her excitement, causing the librarian to frown.

But this girl is just so bubbly with bliss that no one can calm her down. Oh, how wound up Grayson is. She starts to tell you how nice it is that she's finally got your attention 'cause she's always wanted to talk to you and be your friend. At first you feel good. Wow—you never realized she felt that way. But little by little, the real story starts to surface.

Turns out she only wants to know how the Habitat for Humanity meeting went. Not that she's actually interested in the club—it's just that this past Saturday there was a planning meeting and even some of the top jocks showed, including Jake, the hottest guy in school. Afterward they all stopped by your house for some grub and some of them stayed late and played basketball with your brother.

In nothing flat, Grayson's true motive for chatting you up rears its head. Turns out she only wants to know what Jake's like up close. She grills you about every little move he made. And when you say you actually didn't stick around for the basketball part—but that Brandi did—Grayson's saccharine smile fades fast. And after saying something lame, she's off, scouting out where Brandi is this moment. And then you hear her using the same lines on Brandi that she used on you: "Wow, it's so great to see you. You're someone I've admired for a long time. . . ." Blah-blah-blah.

Halfway through the day, when you see Grayson and Brandi walking around like best friends, it becomes clear to you what just happened: You just met the Phony.

Dear Dr. Erika:
This girl I know in school acts, like, so cool, 'specially when she's not telling the truth. Fact is, she can lie up a hurricane. When she's late she'll just bat her eyelashes at the teacher and come out with the worst lies after buttering her up. "Oh, Miss Jones, you're my all-time favorite teacher. I've learned so, so much from you. You're turning my whole life around, really, really."

But behind the teachers' backs she's totally diff. She's, like, a mean witch—you know the word I'm thinking. Any rate, she never gets caught. That's what's the worst. She always, like, manages to wriggle out of whatever lies she's been dishing out. Like she's got Teflon skin—nothing sticks. And on top of that, she makes good grades and gets invited to the best parties.

Kimmie, 13

FYI

This chick is tricky! She seems like a fab friend on the surface. She pays lots of attention to you, tells you the nicest things, and talks to you—but *only* when you're in a position to do her some good. When she wants something from you.

Yeah. The friendship Phony is always right by your side or on the phone calling you or e-mailing you, but only when you have cash to spare, a ride to offer, a piece of yummy chocolate cake, a 30 percent–off coupon for the hottest shoe store, homework she can copy, or free tickets to the next hot concert.

Or if your dad suddenly takes a job with Universal Pix. Or you win the national science project contest and some photogs are coming by to take pix of you, and maybe a few friends. Wowee. Then she stands, beaming, right next to you for this photo op. Her whitened teeth outgleam yours!

> There's this girl who's always waiting round till I win a competition and stuff. Then she's like, "Hey, I've always been your best friend, haven't I?" And she tags along to the banquet and whatever. But never when I'm not getting some major prize.
>
> Jamie, 16

This is typical Phony friendship maneuvering. The Phony thinks of other girls only as things she can use to get what she wants and where she wants to be. When you're successful, she gloms on to you like gum on the bottom of your shoe and becomes fast friends with you. But she fades away even faster if your fame doesn't last. If another girl outshines you, she switches allegiances.

So face it. A Phony isn't a friend, only a good-time gal pal who likes to sponge off your good fortune. Then she ditches you for another, hotter girl or a new big name. In her opinion. But it never takes long for the Phony to join a new throng. There's always another girl who gets elected prom queen or head cheerleader or class prez.

And that may or may not be you. So, be careful around this Phony friend who's really just a hanger-on. If you have a bad day or week, she's long gone.

What's her real friendship potential? Not much, unless you win the Mega Millions lottery. Every week!

Freedom High School, USA

Ushi is an only child and close to her dad. He always tells her that connections are everything. Everything! Remember that. That's why he's struggling so hard—he has to. He's an immigrant but changed his last name and doesn't speak with an accent, so nobody knows. And in school when they're studying world literature and are reading a story from Ushi's dad's home country—usually it's about some dumb farmer who struggles, struggles, struggles all his life only to be cheated by a city slicker, or about a boy who suffered after a war disaster—Ushi ducks down, feeling heat rise to her neck and face. She hopes nobody in class suddenly looks at her and mentions her dad's overseas background.

Nobody does.

And that's such a relief. And that's also the reason Ushi loves school so much. She's not a slacker like so many girls. A lot of them are doing only enough to get by. It's because they don't know what's it's like in other places in the world. They take stuff for granted. But not her. Ushi has a long-range plan. She's going to get a master's in pharmacy and make big bucks. Actually, she'd like to become a doctor.

You got to have connections in the U.S. Remember that. Ushi does, and how—she does everything she can to be connected with the right people.

She arrives at school early, finds a place near the front office to wait for her friends. While she does, she studies the latest flashing school bulletin. That is a giant computer screen on which the up-to-the minute awards and honors of the "school family" are announced every day. Like, who came in first in the conference track and field meet. Who gave the best speech at the annual Community Civic Club convention. Who was chosen to represent the school at Girls State or Governor's School?

Ah, here are the names: Meghan, Anna, and Kaitlyn.

Darn, not her. But of course it couldn't be. She's just a soph and not even in track or speech class. And you have to be a junior to get picked for the other stuff.

But Ushi's no slouch. She was second VP of the ninth grade and once got honorable mention for a poster. Of course, she'll do much better this year. Has to.

Now several other girls enter the lobby and say hi to her. She greets them back in a lukewarm tone. They're nice, but she's holding out for something better. Ushi talks with them while watching the door. Finally, she spots Meghan in front of the school, climbing out of her mom's car. Ushi flies out the door, leaving the other girls in midsentence, so she can help Meghan tote some of her stuff. As Ushi escorts Meghan into school, she beams.

Before zooming off, Meghan's mom asks Ushi to remind Meghan to drink plenty of water. So now Ushi has an *in*. Hey, she's like Meghan's trainer, sort of. Or like her best friend. If Meghan wins again, maybe she'll get some credit too. For sure. Or maybe she'll try hanging out with Anna and Kaitlyn. She can be friends with all of them. All their moms are members of this way-prominent women's club that hands out scholarships, and Ushi's determined to get noticed by them. One way or another.

FAST FRIENDSHIP FITNESS TEST

Could You Be a Phony Friend Magnet?

1 You just won first place in the school poetry contest. All of a sudden, the Phony wants to sit next to you in English class. She asks you to hang out after school. She invites you to her parties. You know that there's a big term paper coming up that she wants you to help her with. You:

a. Know that she's just using you, but you agree to help her anyway. You don't want people to think that you're a selfish jerk for not helping her.

b. Totally help her out. You like all of the attention you're getting from her. Besides, if you don't help her out, she'll just move on to someone else, and then you'll be left out.

c. Know that she's a total fake, so you decide to put her in her place. All the time she's acting super sugary-nice to you, you do the same back to her. You act like her best friend in the whole world. And she has no idea that, all the while, when you're supposed to be helping her, you're giving her all of the wrong answers and information! That'll teach her not to use people! So what if she flunks English? She deserves it.

d. Realize that she's being ultrafriendly because she wants something from you. From experience, you know that she's going to use you, as she has used other girls in the past, so you're polite but you decide to keep your distance. Getting too close to the Phony always leaves you out in the cold.

2 Until last week, you had the lead in the school play, and the Phony was acting like your best friend in the world. But then you broke your ankle at soccer practice, and now you can't be in the play and you have a big, bulky cast! The Phony totally drops you and becomes best buds with the new lead. You're suddenly invisible. You:

a. Stay that way. It would have been fun to do the play, but you're more the quiet type anyway. And even though you're secretly crushed that the Phony ditched you, you'd never let her know that. So, you blend into the woodwork and stay out of the other girls' way. You're a lost cause anyway.

b. Tag along with the Phony and her new friend wherever they go. Even though you're not in the play anymore, you still want to get at least *some* of the attention.

c. "Accidentally" spill orange soda all over the Phony's brand-new white skirt at lunch as she sits chatting with your replacement in the play. Hey—it's hard to walk with your bulky cast, and you just lost your balance!

d. Let it roll off your back. You know that she's got a rep for using people, and you don't let it bother you. You have a group of friends who love and support you no matter what, so you don't let the Phony's about-face get you down.

3 You can't believe it, but your name got picked in a surprise drawing and you get to go on a shopping spree and take a friend with you. Suddenly, the Phony is your new pal. She starts sitting with you at

lunch and she even invites you to her sleepover. Once you get there, she's acting all super nice and asks if she can go with you on the shopping spree. You:

a. Avoid answering her—you really wanted to take your best friend, but the Phony is being pushy and you're afraid to say no to her because then she might stop talking to you.

b. Tell her she can come. So what if you already promised Briana, your best friend since the second grade, that she could go? You can blow her off—it's no big deal.

c. Act really excited about taking her with you. Then you give her the wrong time . . . and the wrong store.

d. Tell her that you're taking your best friend with you, but invite her over for a postshopping-spree pizza party. Who knows? Maybe if you make an effort to ask her to hang out, she'll realize that it's cool to have real friends around instead of fickle friends.

4 The Phony in your group has started to exclude one of your friends just because she doesn't have as much money as some of the others in your group. You:

a. Tell your friend, in private, that you'll continue to stand by her. But not this week, because the Phony has a lot going on at her house and you've got to hustle on over there—you don't want to get kicked out of the group, too.

b. Drop her as quickly as you can. You've worked too hard to become a part of this group, and you know if you want to stay in the group, you've got to follow the Phony's lead. You can't let anyone or anything drag you down.

c. Spread a schoolwide rumor about the Phony that ousts her from every possible group in the entire school. Never mentioning her name but leaving no doubt about her identity, you publish your masterpieces on the Net or in the school paper's gossip column. Sure, the truth hurts, especially by the time you're done dishing it all out.

d. Talk to the girls in your crowd about what friendship really means—to be there for one another in terrific and tough times. You try to help everyone see that you should be real friends who are supportive and loving, no matter what. But if the Phony continues to be unkind, you'll distance yourself from her. You're friends with girls because you like them, not because of how rich they are.

Now it's time to find out your FQ: Tally your answers. How many A's, B's, C's, and D's do you have?

3 or 4 A's, check out Answer 1.
3 or 4 B's, check out Answer 2.
3 or 4 C's, check out Answer 3.
3 or 4 D's, check out Answer 4.

If you have a mixture of A's, B's, C's, and D's, look at all the answers. Obviously, there's a bit of everything in you, which is fab. Now, can you work on having a little less of the Answer 1 attitude and a little more of the Answer 4 attitude?

Answers

1 Fearful Friend

You're too easily impressed and intimidated by all the Phony baloney. Keep your eyes wide open and try to recognize the real friends from the fake friends. Real friends aren't just skin deep—they'll be with you no matter what, so don't drop them just because you're fearful of the Phony. The Phony will only be around for so long, but a true girlfriend can stick around forever.

Copy Katrina

Hey, girl! What's wrong with keeping it real once in a while? You don't have to let another girl tell you how to act, especially when her motives are flaky and fakey. Why do you let someone else define you? You're no one's imitation or carbon copy. You're a real girl with a mind of your own. Use it or lose it!

3 Mean Queen

You're a girl who's not afraid to speak her mind, but that's no reason to be unkind! Why do you use your bravery to be cruel, when you could use it to be a good friend? It's as if your life depended on making A's in one-upmanship. You've got a strong voice and it's great that you make it heard. Instead of using it to flush out the Phony, why not use it to help your friends?

4 Real Deal

You enjoy having friends and lots of them but not when it means getting used by somebody. Good for you. Sure, you may have fallen for the Phony's act once or twice, but that's no reason not to be nice. Keep up the good work—you're a fab friend to all those around you—and that's the best you can be.

PHONY FACTORS

What Should You Know about the Phony?

A Phony is unsure of herself and her values. Therefore, she's after what she thinks she's missing—something that she thinks she can obtain by using others. That's why she tries to aggrandize herself. That's why she latches on to other girls, in hopes of being a part of their shiny world. That wouldn't be bad if only she'd stick with them. But since there's always another girl with more to offer—in the opinion of the Phony—she's constantly on the move to upgrade her friends. So, what else should you know about the Phony?

- ☑ To get where she wants, she uses any means at her disposal. She can be an out-and-out fibber or liar in word and deed. She acts one way one day, the opposite the next. So watch her carefully—it might seem like she's sincere—then she disappears!
- ☑ She changes her attitude, her style, and her interests according to who she's trying to fit in with at the moment. Try to

remember, her actions really have nothing to do with you, so try not to measure your self-worth by how the Phony is treating you. She's a slick chick.

☑ It's hard to get close to the Phony because nobody knows who she really is. She's like a human chameleon who at times forgets all the roles she's already played and all the promises she made but never kept. But who knows? Maybe if a real-deal girl like you shows her what good friends are like, she might come around. But proceed with caution and stay true to your other fab friends—you don't want to end up the Phony's fool!

FIRST AID

What You Should Do about the Phony

So, now that you've got the scoop on the Phony, what can you do about her? Check out the list below for some quick tips.

1. Don't believe everything she says. Just treat her like you would any demo perfume spritzer at the mall—she may be charming and disarming, but what she wants most is a sale. The Phony also is charming and disarming, but only because she wants something as well. Not a sale, but a fat slice of your fame and fortune. Or an intro to someone else or a step up, even if it means she has to step on your back.
2. Whenever you get the chance, tell her you like her just the way she is. That may shock her, but it may help her to realize how fabulous real friendship can be. Let her know that she doesn't have to pretend around you—she can be herself and it's okay.
3. Do your best to have a positive influence on the Phony, but don't count on the Phony to be your good friend. She's entertaining to watch but she isn't capable of being a solid pal unless she does a major self-makeover. Until then, her insecurities make her unreliable, changeable, and fickle—like a breeze coming from different directions.

FIRST PERSON

How I Handled It-Sandi's Real-Life Story

When I started eleventh grade, everything went crazy at my school. All of a sudden, everyone started talking about the PSAT and the SATs. And everyone was talking like if you didn't do good on them, your life was over. Really over. Because you couldn't go to college then. But really it was said that you couldn't get into a good college unless you made, like, a 1600 on those tests. Girls were going, "If I don't get into UNC-Chapel Hill or Duke, I'll just, like, die!"

So, it was, like, a constant contest of who would be first. Then this new girl moved to our class and she was real nice to me and my friends, especially before a test. She always wanted to hang out. Then one day she totally ignored us. Turned out her cousin had the same teachers the year before and kept all his notes, so she just used his notes and blew us off. Then to study, she used her cousin's old quizzes and was always way ahead. This wasn't fair to the rest of us, having to start from scratch and not knowing what would be covered and all. But she never shared. And suddenly her only friends were girls who had already been accepted at Ivy League schools. None of the rest of us counted anymore.

So, one day in gym, we just went into her backpack and took out all her cheat sheets. We tossed them in the trash. That night, she called each of us and asked, "Did you see anyone messing with my backpack?" And we said, no. No. No! She said she'd be watching us like a hawk. And if any of our grades went up drastically, she'd know it was us! Guess I'm just going to have to miss a couple of questions on each test from now on. On purpose. 'Cause I really kept the most important papers.—Sandi, 17

CHICK-POINT

Grade the Girls

F ✱
D ✱✱
C ✱✱✱
B ✱✱✱✱
A ✱✱✱✱✱

Chick Grades: No stars this time!

A big fat chick-minus to all the girls who participated in the theft. Granted, it wasn't fair that Ms. Phony Newcomer kept using her cousin's work and didn't even bother to take her own notes. And that she hogged the old quizzes to study by. But what you should have done is inform the teacher anonymously that his old tests were being used, and ask him to update his exams. Even better would be if he'd make copies of all old tests available to anyone interested.

But no, no. You guys weren't just out for fairness. You wanted revenge. Blood. So you stole and then you lied about it. So who's the real Phony here? And as for you, Sandi, you were the phoniest of the Phonies. You kept the prized papers all for yourself. You deserve a chick-minus-minus-minus.

Dear Diary

Have you ever been envious of a friend's clothes, looks, life? It's okay if you have. We all have. But then you probably realized that being envious is a lousy feeling, one you're so much better off without. Because when you're consumed with envy, you're disregarding what you're standing for, what you represent—which is a whole lot—and you're overvaluing what another girl has.

The Grass Is Always Greener

Even though it may seem like other girls have it all, try to think about what's great in your own life. Chances are, there are probably girls who look at you and wish they had your life, too! So, instead of getting angry or sad, try to think of the good things instead. Count your blessings. How can you do that? Write them down, of course! So get out your trusty diary and write down everything you're thankful for. You've got three minutes.

Now look at the names of your friends that you've listed in earlier entries. Think about the fact that all these girls have lots of blessings too, and that together as a group, you can amp up those blessings even more.

So, if you think your clothes are all wrong or that your hairdo is sooo last year, then pick a friend from the list who could help you spice up your wardrobe or update your tresses. Write a paragraph about it. How would you want her to help you? Next, think about a couple of things you could help her with and write a paragraph about that. What could you do for her? It worked for Carrie:

> This friend of mine's just awful with purses. She'd tote a grocery bag if I'd let her. And I'm awful with hair and think any ratty rubber band is rad. Well, I got her to switch to a supercool purse, and she got me these hot ribbons.
>
> Carrie, 14

Good job, girls. Friends help each other in many ways. Once you all combine your great girl qualities together, there are no limits to what you can do!

FRIEND SPOTTING

The Phony

- ☑ The Phony is always playing musical chairs with friends. You'll see her constantly on the go from one friendship experience to another. In the course of one week, she'll be best friends with you, then another girl, then a third one. She never keeps the same friends for long, because she's always looking for the next best thing.
- ☑ You can spot a Phony by the turbulent wake she leaves behind. Since the Phony is always moving on, her words are nothing more than empty phrases—she often break promises when she sees a better opportunity coming along.
- ☑ The Phony jumps from group to group, girl to girl—while always being on the lookout for some celeb to latch on to, or someone to butter up, or how to wrangle an invitation to the next hot get-together.

Rx for Phony Probs or Phoniness

No one is 100 percent "real" 100 percent of the time, okay? There are times when you may find yourself acting like a Phony. Maybe you want to shield a friend from something harsh, like the absolute truth about her butchered 'do and so you tell a harmless little white lie and assure her that she's making a fabulous fashion statement. But please, never let the Phony baloney get the best of you.

1. When you find yourself tempted to tell a lie, ask yourself why. What are you gaining by lying? Why not stick to the facts?
2. Do your best to tell the truth without being hurtful. Instead of telling your friend that her nightmare lime-green-and-purple outfit looks great, try being truthful but tactful. Say, "Not bad, but I think your tan-and-black outfit makes you look even better." That way, you're helping your friend without hurting her.
3. Remember, flattery will get you nowhere. If you butter up only the top chicks in your school with schmooze, you lose—your identity, your realness, your good friend ability. Don't ever Phony up to some girls. Be a sincere friend, a good friend. Being a hypocrite isn't it.

A girl on my baton-twirling squad is such a phony. When she doesn't want to practice, she always develops cramps and goes home. But later you see her at the mall with Tiffany. "What's up?" you ask. And she goes, "Oh, I got better and they had this sale at Nordstrom's we couldn't miss . . ." Baloney! With a capital B.

Chandra, 15

Chicks Mix

What you want, what you deserve, is real friends, reliable friends. And to improve your chances of finding them, you have to be willing to make the effort to start the process. The good news is that making real friends is often cumulative. When you find one real good friend, you find lots. So that's what you'll do from now on—have your eyes open to any real friend. Maybe in the past you thought that friends have to be exactly like you, act like you, and look like you. That's soooo not true!

Class Actions

Now go over your interactions with your friends today. Replay your chats in your mind. Reread the e-mails you sent out. Remember the texting you did. Did you tell it like it is, was, will be, most of the time? Or did you just mush and gush about what you thought others would like to hear? Then rewrite one or two of your baloney comments into truthful ones. Next time, use them. Look at your friendship quest as an adventure and reach out to girls. Start speaking to girls from different backgrounds—from foreign countries, from the opposing soccer team, from another part of town. From all over. Stop limiting yourself to just one particular type.

> The qualities I look for in my friends have nothing to do with their looks. It's kindness, smarts, being outgoing and trustworthy, wild, crazy, friendly, and talkative—that's what matters to me, not the color of their skin or the way they dress.
>
> Amy, 14

Amy is right! You'll be amazed at how empowering it is to be open and welcoming to all kinds of girls who have true hearts and good intentions. Again, what they look like is not important. What's inside of them is. You're looking for girls with lots of friendship potential who will stand by you and you by them.

Never mind what packages they come wrapped in.

Chick-Mate

Phony friends exist everywhere and are easy to scout out. Just watch what they do—to you and other girls. Be nice to them, but don't let yourself get caught up in their game.

- When the Phony is open to a heart-to-heart, tell her what's bothering you about her fakeness, but don't expect instant change. It's hard for a Phony to have to face the fact that she's treating other girls like stepping-stones in her world.

If she is willing to hear you out and tries to change, then there's hope for her. Perhaps you can give her a chance.

- Otherwise, cool your friendship with her. You are a wonderful, powerful girl with so many potentially great friends just waiting for you. So that's what you do. You concentrate on girls with real-friend futures.

This girl in my school always clings to me when I have something she wants. But never for long. When I have a problem, she's, like, changed her cell phone number.

Angeline, 17

- Overall, you just don't have time to spend on a girl who is using you. You've got so much to offer and you don't need the Phony's behavior dragging you down. The problem is that the phony is often an Oscar-type actress, so you tend to believe her, sure. So watch for these surefire Phony signs:
    - She changes friends constantly—almost like a game of musical chairs. Except she's always changing for more popular girls . . . or girls who have better stuff.
    - She moves on to a new group of friends without caring about the girls she left behind in her sneaky social climb.
    - She speaks in an insincere tone of voice—you can almost tell that she doesn't mean it.
    - She smiles at you with her mouth and not with her eyes.

So don't ever be fooled by a Phony. Talk to her, sure. Light chatter is best. But if you feel like she's deceiving you, trust your gut. She most likely is. The truth is that her friendship potential isn't only low, it can also be detrimental to you.

Instead of bringing out the best in you, the Phony, if you let her, could bring out the worst in you. Or drag and sag you down. But understanding the Phony and learning from her behavior will bring out the ultrabest in you—always. So enjoy and profit from this experience. It'll help you so much along the way if and when you learn to discern and disarm the Phonies now.

FRIENDSHIP RATING SCALE

The Friendship Rating Scale goes from 1 to 10 (with 1 being way low and 10 being tops), which will help you make up your mind about which girls are hot friendship-wise and which for sure are not. You'll see a Friendship Rating at the end of each chapter!

Friendship Finder

Overall, the Phony is a 2, 3, or 4. But the final decision is yours—so turn to the Friendship Rating Scale to find out for sure.

1	Kick yourself for ever thinking about trying to be friends with her.
2	Serious waste of time.
3	May be a waste of time.
4	One more try can't hurt.
5	If you feel like investing more time, that's fine.
6	Keep trying to be her friend.
7	Try harder.
8	Try harder and smarter.
9	Put making friends with this girl on the top of your list.
10	Really strive to be friends with her. Then you will thrive.

Dwelling on the negative simply contributes to its power. –Shirley MacLaine

Chapter 4

The Enemy

n., s.: A friend failure, a toxic and bad chick, a kick-to-the-curb and get-away-from-quick chick; can be wicked, antagonistic, sadistic, fanatic, chaotic, cryptic, traumatic, problematic, vandalistic. Watch out!

What Makes a Girl an Enemy?

While the Airhead, the Me-Me Chick, and the Phony all run low on friendship potential, the Enemy is the worst. She's the most scary girl you'll meet, and the one to really stay clear of. Whenever possible, make a detour around her because she's after you. So watch your back!

Unfortunately this Enemy girl exists in every group, even though she may be difficult to spot at first. She's a negative force. She can be disruptive and destructive.

> I think friendship is just a made-up thing that doesn't exist. Sorta like Santa Claus or the Tooth Fairy, you know?
>
> Ella, 14

That's exactly how the Enemy thinks—that friendship is nothing, just a figment of the imagination or a way bad joke. And that's why the Enemy is someone to be worried about. You better believe it.

Dear Dr. Erika:
This girl has a camera phone and took a picture of me one day when I was wearing a miniskirt and was bending down to pick up my pen. Then she had the nerve to post my picture all over the Net. She thought it was so funny! I went to the teacher and told her. She took it to the office, but they said unless I had more info, they couldn't do anything about it. And now everyone is looking at me and whispering and I'm so embarrassed. It's gross! I feel so bad now, like I've been run over by a truck. I'm aching everywhere and don't know what to do.

Ryanne, 15

FYI

Enemies are adversaries or people against you. In the girl world, Enemies are girls who do bad things—to other girls and, in the end, to themselves. These girls can take an instant dislike to you—for no good reason at all! It may be because you have something they want. Or because you look like they'd like to look. Or because you have a talent they don't. Or it can be something like the way you talk or the way you walk. Or your height or weight or because you're never late.

It's often difficult to discern why the Enemy has targeted you or your group. Often there's no particular reason why the Enemy is so filled with dislike, even hate, against you and your friends. At times this dislike or hate is quite obvious. At other times the Enemy pretends to be part of your crew while secretly scheming against you.

The fact is, those types of girls don't want to be friends. They want to be Enemies.

Friendship is nothing to me. Just something to squash like a nasty bug. Yuck.

Melanie, 14

Sad to say, but there really are some girls that feel like Melanie does. To them, friendship is meaningless. Sometimes it's even worse. Maybe because they've never had a friend or because they were once betrayed by a friend. Maybe that's why they take it out on others.

Maybe as far back as they can remember, no person has ever been there for them to rely on, to depend on. That's why they can't trust, and trust is a must in being friends.

> There are girls that take a look at you, size you up in an instant, decide they hate you and then do their best to make you crash. And then they sit on you! And it's tough to get out from under them.
>
> Avienne, 17

Freedom High School, USA

As soon as Dorie strides into the gym where she usually waits before the first bell, the atmosphere changes. All the other girls stop talking and laughing. They watch her fearfully. And that's such a great feeling. Dorie just loves it. And she deserves it. She's worked hard to obtain this status of being the worst chick around.

So, of course, nobody ever dares say anything about her. And when she wants a seat in the bleachers, or a whole row, or any seat in the cafeteria, she gets it. All she has to do is make her way toward any spot in a room, and the other girls scramble. Some girls even dust off a chair for her—those shrimps and wimps.

They're all like what Dorie used to be like before she was twelve. They are young girls who are naïve, believe anything and everything. Little lambs really. But not her. She's all grown up and on fast forward.

Hey, it's a cruel world out there and only the tough survive.

Today Dorie's posse, who proudly call themselves The Drastics, have taken over the lobby of the Athletic Department. Dozens of other girls have arrived early too, to talk to coaches or pick up permission forms to ride on the activity bus or van, or to show their report cards—you gotta have at least a C average to stay on a team.

No sweat for Dorie. She's got the teachers intimidated, especially the young ones. They wouldn't dare flunk her. Uh-uh. Nobody hassles her 'cause who likes their car keyed, even if it's an old clunker like most of those teachers drive?

The other girls jump up and give Dorie and her crew the best seats—the padded ones in the lobby near the drink machines.

Smiling, she plunks down in the choicest spot—a big armchair—leans back, and surveys her buds. They consist of all the stars in track, b-ball, and softball. It's a super bunch and so lively, loud. This being Monday, they have so much to catch up on.

They spill and dish about how their folks hassled them over the weekend. Dorie smiles; nobody hassles her at home. Dad's always so silent. So she pretty much comes and goes as she pleases. But while she smiles, there's a stab of pain in her heart. Oh, if only there were somebody to question her comings and goings. For a second, Dorie flashes back to her twelfth birthday. It's like it happened yesterday. She got up way early, so excited about her big day. Then she saw her dad's face in the deserted kitchen. He looked gray, aged, like his cheeks had fallen. Turned out that during the night, Mom had taken off. No note, no good-bye, no nothing. She was just—gone. Later, she surfaced in Europe. Where exactly Dorie didn't know. Dad never mentioned her again.

But ever since Dorie's been asking herself what she's done to make her mom do that. She figures that she must have done something wrong to make her mom leave without saying good-bye. And since Dad won't talk to her about it, she just knows that he blames her, too.

At first, she used to cry all night back then, wishing she knew what she'd done wrong so she could understand what had happened. Actually these days she never thinks about her mother—except for days like this when she's forging "mom" signatures for the other girls.

As she finishes signing the last form, the new girl in school is walking by and they make eye contact.

"What do you want, fatso?" Dorie snaps at her, and is gratified as the girl winces and hurries away.

FAST FRIENDSHIP FITNESS TEST

Could You Be an Enemy Magnet?

1 You're in algebra class when you notice the Enemy trying to get your attention from across the room. You:

a. Duck your head down and pretend you don't see her. She's probably just trying to pick on you, anyway. You're sure that no matter what, she'll embarrass you. So you keep tragedy at bay by playing "the invisible game" and hope that she gives up and targets someone else.

b. Know that you should wait until after class to see what she wants, but instead you pass her a note. One problem: The teacher catches you and gives you detention. Great! Now you have detention *and* you have to suffer all the teasing from the Enemy and her crowd.

c. Know that she's been in lots of trouble with the teacher lately, so you decide to get her in a little more. You smile sweetly at the Enemy, then raise your hand and tell the teacher in your best "perfect student" voice that the Enemy is disrupting you by making faces and noises and that you can't concentrate on the lesson. You even smile through the Enemy's dirty looks. She's usually all talk anyway. And whatever revenge she plans—it was worth it.

d. Wait until after class and ask her if there's something she needs. Turns out, she wanted to tell you that she likes your shoes! How weird, right? Even the Enemy has good days and bad days. You thank her and then make your way to your next class. You decide that the next time you see her, you'll give her a compliment, too.

2 You've been getting some evil-mails. You can't be 100 percent sure, but you're pretty certain they're from the Enemy at your school. Ever since you started getting these e-mails, when you see the Enemy at school, she and her friends are whispering and giggling in your direction. You:

a. Use the Delete key and whistle while you work. That's what this key is for: delete, delete, delete. Ta-da, all done.

Your incoming-mail file and screen are always super nice and clean.

b. Are just so thrilled that you're getting e-mail. Actually it's not that you like this kind, but it's better than nothing and you can count on it. There's always something waiting for you in your inbox. Aren't you getting way popular?

c. Get her personal e-mail address and put it on every ridiculous mailing list there is. You'll make sure her inbox is flooded with so much spam she won't even be able to get to her real messages. You also send a really sexy e-mail message from her account to your really un-sexy principal! You'll make sure your e-mails are the most evil of all!

d. Write back to her and tell her to stop evil-mailing you. Then print out all the nasty e-mails and keep them so you have a record. If her evil-mailing persists, give copies of the e-mails to your parents, teachers, or another adult you trust. Enough is enough!

3 The Enemy in your class is selected as the captain of your volleyball team. She immediately tells you that she's not letting you play. Ever. You:

a. Figure there's nothing else you can do. She clearly hates you, but you feel powerless against her. Anyway, maybe there are other sports you can switch to. You heard that the speed basket-weaving team is short several members.

b. Become her faithful little servant instead of fighting to play. You've always considered volleyball your sport, but so what? Instead of playing, you run to get her favorite brand of designer water; bring her uniform all nice, fresh, and starched; and do any other errands she asks you to. Hey, you may not be playing, but at least you're being recognized and appreciated by the captain!

c. Know exactly what she is up to—sabotaging you. And that's ★#!+! unacceptable. So, on the day of the conference match, you go out of your way to fix her. You "lose" her lucky pair of shoes, the ones she's been wearing every game and is so superstitious about. "Revenge is mine" is your mantra. Of course all the girls on the team will suffer, but so what?

d. Practice as hard or harder than ever before. You always try. The other girls will appreciate your efforts, and the coach will recognize your talents. You know that you're a strong player, and as the captain, she can't make a decision to keep you from playing. You even have a talk with the coach to share your concerns, and you stay calm and trust that the Enemy's decision will be overruled. She may be a bully, but she doesn't run your life!

4 You overhear the Enemy in class as she brags about her plans to totally embarrass the prom queen. Every day she details more and more how she's going to do it. You:

a. Are so glad you're not on the homecoming court—not that you'd ever stand a chance of getting elected. You *are* on the decorations committee, but you quit immediately so nobody will get mad at you. You're washing your hands of the whole thing. No controversy for you!

b. Join in with some of the Enemy's discussions of preposterous prom plans when you have class with her. But when you're in class with members of the homecoming court, you never say a word to them about the Enemy's plans. Instead, you talk to them about their dresses, their dates, and their plans for after prom. You see no reason to rock the boat—after all, none of this really involves you, right? If you play innocent, you can't get hurt.

c. Get a group of friends together and create a Society for the Prevention of Cruelness to Prom Queens. You make Wanted posters of the Enemy and her crew and post them all over the school—anonymously, of course! You're sick and tired of the Enemy and her antics. Once the teachers and the homecoming court see the posters, the Enemy will probably be banned from prom. Serves her right!

d. Tip off the homecoming court in a general way, just so they're aware that something is going on. Since you're on the decorations committee, you also find a way to mention the plan to the prom committee teachers without mentioning any names. You aren't in the mood to get involved in drama—you just want to go to the prom and have the best time ever.

Now it's time to find out your FQ: Tally your answers. How many A's, B's, C's, and D's do you have?

3 or 4 A's, check out Answer 1.
3 or 4 B's, check out Answer 2.
3 or 4 C's, check out Answer 3.
3 or 4 D's, check out Answer 4.

If you have a mixture of A's, B's, C's, and D's, look at all the answers. Obviously, there's a bit of everything in you, which is fab. Now, can you work on having a little less of the Answer 1 attitude and a little more of the Answer 4 attitude?

Answers

1 Fraidy Baby

If you could live by yourself in a walled-in garden and never have to meet other girls, you'd be doing great. But that's unrealistic. So how're you ever going to learn to deal with the girl world if you always withdraw into your safe corner? You've got lots of good things inside of you just waiting to come out, so stop shaking like a leaf and turn over a new leaf. Next time, speak your mind! You might be surprised at how much better you feel.

2 Enemy Enabler

To contribute to something good is good. To contribute to something bad is—you. Sounds harsh but true. So ask yourself: Is that what you want—to aid and abet the enemy at your school? It's great to feel accepted into a group—but this definitely isn't the way to do it, girl! It only takes away from the real you inside—the great girl you were meant to be.

3 Helen of Trouble

On one hand, it's great that you try to fight against the Enemy's ways, but why do you automatically turn into a wicked warrior anytime you see a girl doing worse stuff than you? Even though your actions have good intentions, they're really no better than those of the mean chicks in your school. Life isn't about besting the worst girl in your school. It's about being your best and helping other girls be their best.

4 Fab Friend

Yay! Yippee and good for you. You know how to stay out of the drama, but you also recognize that whenever you overhear rumors of bullying and pranking, you have a responsibility. You're a girl who's determined to make the world a good place and fun for everyone. But bad apples can spoil the whole bunch, so you help to weed them out.

ENEMY FACTORS

What Should You Know about the Enemy?

The enemy is a girl who claims to be your friend but isn't—at all. It's as simple as that. She's not your friend. She's your opponent, your adversary, and your detractor. In short, she's against you. She comes in three types.

The Pain Promoter

The Pain Promoter is the kind of girl who doesn't actually ever do anything to hurt you, but she'll encourage others to say mean things to you or act mean to you. And then she tells you about the mean stuff being said about you. Or she will egg on the mean doers to a higher degree of meanness. She's a girl who enjoys hurting other girls—but only from a distance. That way when things hit the fan, she can always say, *Didn't do it.* Yet she did—by stirring up the pot of pain. And by contributing her time to really turn up the heat. This enemy often comes dressed in sheep's clothing, but beware, her bad influence is always there. And sometimes, this type of enemy was once a good friend, but no more.

> My friends used to be real nice and then something changed. Now I always have this bad feeling 'cause they're always talking about ripping someone off, screwing someone over, excuse the expression, getting back at other girls big-time and doing stuff we're not supposed to do. And when I point out that that's wrong, they laugh and call me a sissy or a wimp.
>
> Julia, 14

The Evil Doer

This girl will come right out and tell you she hates you. Why is anyone's guess. It may be a reaction to something she heard the Pain Promoter (see above) say that you said, which of course you didn't say, or was taken out of context. Or it may be just because her own life is so rough and tough that she's like a wounded and cornered animal. Feeling such agony, she lashes out at anyone passing by. And you just happen to be that person. So always keep in mind that you're not the reason a girl is the Enemy.

The Frenemy

This girl is the absolute worst! She's the Frenemy. That means, a former friend who turns into an Enemy. But she hides her true feelings as she targets you sneakily. She smiles in your face while busily sharpening her claws. Or getting out a dagger and polishing it. Then she stabs you in the back when you least expect it. But now you know, so you can either put on armor or reach out and disarm her. Either way, you're the empowered one.

FIRST AID

What You Should Do about the Enemy

Just because the Enemy is there dishing out her mean stuff doesn't mean that you're just going to have to take it. No way! What you and your real friends need to do is watch your backs. Here's how:

1. Once you have identified the Enemy in your group or school—that is, the girl who's always bringing you all the dirt supposedly dished by other girls about you and then pushes and prods you until she's extracted a way mad reaction from you, which she then delivers ASAP back to her gang—disarm her. How? By nixing her and her bad news crew. Tell anyone reporting to you what nasty stuff is being said about you, "Oh, the price of fame. Guess people will talk." Otherwise give no other reaction.
2. And for sure, don't escalate the gossip war by slinging your own brand of rumors and innuendoes. Name calling isn't cool. Even if it's in self-defense. The best weapon is full self-esteem ahead. And, of course, your armor of real friends. They're the sure cure. You are mean-chick-proof with all the friends this book will help you to get by the time you finish reading.

FIRST PERSON

How I Handled It-Kate's Real-Life Story

The absolute worst disaster of my whole life was last week. I was trying out for the basketball team and was sooo scared that I wouldn't make it. So many other athletic girls, especially Mollie and Paula, are way better than me and had been, like, going to all these college-type summer sports camps. So I told my friends about being real nervous about not making the cut.

They said, Hey, no sweat, chill, girl. You're better than those chicks.

On the first day of tryouts, what a relief—Mollie and Paula didn't even show up for practice. See, we have this rule that you have to attend all practice sessions that run for two whole weeks.

But with my biggest competitors not even appearing, I felt so relieved and really showed my stuff. I actually rocked—I hit five three-pointers.

After those tryouts, I was pretty sure I was gonna head up the final list—yay.

But when I told my friends about it, they smirked. They were like, "We e-mailed Mollie and Paula a revised tryout schedule; we changed the dates, he-he. Now, what else do you need us to do?" I couldn't believe what they did, but I don't want to give up my chance to be on the team.—Kate, 16

CHICK-POINT

Grade the Girls

F ✱
D ✱✱
C ✱✱✱
B ✱✱✱✱
A ✱✱✱✱✱

Chick Grades: ✱✱✱

Hello, Kate, c'mon. Let's not worry about getting any chick points right now. You're in the middle of a disaster.

Sure, at first you didn't know what your friends were up to. But as soon as they admitted sending the wrong info to Paula and Mollie, why didn't you fess up? Think about it. Sure, it may seem like your friends are looking out for you, but they are actually acting like Enemies to Paula and Mollie. Instead of giving you the fab friend support you needed, they've ruined your rep. How long do you think it'll take for the coach to get to the bottom of the stars' absences?

Not long, bet on it.

You need to do a little friendship footwork of your own and think about how "real" your friends really are. Their behavior was sad, bad, and totally unacceptable. And listen: Keeping quiet a second longer will only draw you farther into their spite spiral.

Dear Diary

Okay, now it's time to write about all of the feelings you have about the Enemy in your life (if there is one!). Grab your fave pen and let's get down to business.

Exorcising the Enemy

You probably know this by now, but writing about your feelings is one of the best ways to deal with them. So this little exercise will help you exorcise any bad feelings you have about the Enemy.

Write down anything mean an Enemy has ever done to you. Or said to you. Or to your friends. Just let all the negative feelings travel from wherever you keep them deep inside you to your hand, fingers, fingertips, and from there into your pen or pencil. Let it fill your clean sheet of paper. Whatever nasty or cruel or rude or crude thing ever happened to you—write it all out—get it all down.

Some of these things could even be from some of your friends, or even Frenemies, who have hurt you in the past.

Looking to the Future

Once you feel like you've gotten through lots of your feelings, turn over the paper and think of the millions of nice girls that exist out there in the girl world. And picture them as your personal army, your no-lie allies. They are all on your side—they've got your back—they'll always fight for you. You probably know a lot of them right now, but there are more to come—girls (and women!) you'll meet in high school or college or even in your job (whoa—that seems like a long way off, right?) who have the potential to be fabulous friends. But for the time being, just imagine them now as they might cluster around you. Imagine the love and support you feel from your friends magnified a thousand times—that is your future! The power of many will trump whatever mean-chick tricks have happened to you.

Now put your pen or pencil aside, sit up straight, and feel strong. Because you are. You now know that in order to cure mean behaviors, you have to surround yourself with friends. Plus, you now know that challenges, even the scariest of enemies, have some plus points. They make you discover things about yourself that can come in handy later. For sure, they reinforce your friend ability. You see, without at least one enemy in your group or club or on your team, you couldn't grow into the brave and independent young woman you are and will continue to be. So, if you're faced with an Enemy or an evil-egger-on or a Frenemy, be glad because they are part of what makes you uniquely, perfectly, specially you.

> Learn from the enemy and leave them, is my motto. I look at what they do and do the exact opposite. More often than not, that's exactly the right thing.
>
> Reese, 15

Great advice, Reese. And Maria has something for you to keep in mind, too:

> Most of all a friend should be a person who won't get me in trouble. That's basic.
>
> Maria, 14

FRIEND SPOTTING

The Enemy

So how can you spot the Enemy and keep yourself safe from her trouble tactics? Here's how:

☑ Be on the lookout for any girl who has violent temper outbursts. Some enemy girls may be good girls otherwise, but they have a mean disposition or are prone to tantrums. If they're three years old, they can get away with it, but if they're older, that's so uncool.

> When a girl who is trouble, I mean trouble with a capital *T*, calls your name, just say "hey" and keep on walking. Don't make it obvious and mean. Keep your manners but don't get too friendly.
>
> Armana, 15

☑ A surefire way to spot the Enemy is by her put-downs. The Enemy will be quick to make the girls around her feel bad—usually by saying mean things to them. So try and steer clear of Enemies—know your Enemies and "no" them.

Never hang out behind the Bojangles parking lot. 'Cause that's where a lot of kids cook up stuff and I don't mean good stuff.

Hallie, 15

☑ The Enemy thrives on fear—that's how she gets all of her power. Can you think of any ways that you can show her you're not afraid of her Enemy antics?

Rx for X-ing out Enemy-osity

Have you ever woken up feeling sooo angry at everyone and anyone crossing your path, 'specially your friends? If so, you're suffering not from animosity but from Enemy-osity. *X* it out fast now. How?

1. Realize that you're having an "anti" day; warn your friends and next day make amends.
2. Plan ahead for times like these. Have a special mag or book handy to flip through when you're just so not you.
3. Know that when dealt with, Enemy-osity can be cured, for sure. So act extra nice to your friends at all times, just do your best, so when you do have an unfriendly attack day, they'll be more likely to overlook it.
4. How wonderful it is that you're a forward-looking girl who has a grip on her future, and that future is going to be so fab. So, you know better than to let any mean-queen teens get in your way and prevent you from progressing.

I don't mind a friend who's having it rough, I help them out. But I don't need anyone covered with loser dust.

Annisette, 14

I know. It sounds so harsh to describe certain girls as covered with "loser dust," but the reality is that you have to—first of all—look out for yourself. If you take all the serious friend failures, including the stirrer-ups, the troublemakers, the malice-minded, and the evil enablers, under your wing, they will really weigh you down. You'll be at a total standstill at best. Or at worst, on a going-back fast track. You will be worse off, no matter what. And that's not what you want. What you want is a sea of smart and similarly minded girls, like a sea of close sisters and real nice girls—all of you being there and helping one another up the ladder to success. Yes!

Chicks Mix

So you be the one to befriend other nice girls. That may mean looking outside your immediate ring of friends and opening the door for girls who so far you hardly ever thought about.

Class Actions

Here's a great thing to do: Adopt a sis. All you do is look around your school, your neighborhood, your youth group at church, synagogue or temple, or mosque, and choose a younger girl to be your mentee. That means you're going to mentor her. See, what's so great about friends is, they don't come just in grade levels. There are several organizations and clubs for youth outreach/mentoring just waiting for you to join in and help out. Rather than find the right one by trial and error by Googling and scouting out the best possibilities on your own, skip on down to the Guidance Department or the librarian and ask them for info, booklets, Web sites, and phone numbers. Then you're in business.

Chick-Mate

Enemies are bad news. Every time. They can outright oppose you. Other times, they undermine you little by little or try to bring you down. Most of the Enemy chicks don't go by the rules, and think girls who do are fools. What they'd like to see is you getting upset or you picking up some of their tough 'tudes. But please don't.

> When I run across a bunch of girls smoking in the bathroom and stuff, I act like I don't notice them and pee fast. Outta there.
>
> Sylvia, 16

- Remember, all Enemies aren't totally and forever mean chicks. Deep inside they may be all right, but they treat you bad or say bad things about you or use bad language nonstop—and for no reason that you can tell. The truth is, their friendship potential is in the minus category and sinking daily.

> This girl I know who is fourteen always wants everyone's attention. She thinks of strange things to do. Mean things. And she brags about what she can get away with and does. Well, I told her to stop it. I was being nice and not calling her a liar—but she got so mad. She blocked both my screen names and refuses to talk to me. And I'm, like, yay. Now I got more time for my real friends.
>
> Wynter, 13

- Having an Enemy and overcoming her can empower you and make you stronger. Think of this as a challenge that stretches you, makes you advance beyond the norm, and brings out your superbest form. Naturally, you can spend time trying to make the Enemy and Frenemy into your friends. Because you're nice and realize that unless helped, they stay in the friendship basement or get worse.
- When you're faced with the Enemy or other mean chicks, ask yourself, Do I have the time and energy to deal with them? You could be leaving all of your real friends out in the cold. Then perhaps all the friendly friends might turn to other girls. And what guarantee do you have that the Enemies who you're trying to get to be nice won't harm you?

So, know that it's always great trying to get new girls to be your friends, but don't spend too much time trying to get the Enemy to be a friend—if you let her, she can drag you down, and that's what we don't want. Not for you, not for anyone else.

FRIENDSHIP RATING SCALE

The Friendship Rating Scale goes from 1 to 10 (with 1 being way low and 10 being tops), which will help you make up your mind about which girls are hot friendship-wise and which for sure are not. You'll see a Friendship Rating at the end of each chapter!

Friendship Finder

On the Friendship Rating Scale, the Enemy is a 1 or, in a few cases, a 2, or in very rare cases, a 3. But what does that mean? Check out the scale to find out.

1	Kick yourself for ever thinking about trying to be friends with her.
2	Serious waste of time.
3	May be a waste of time.
4	One more try can't hurt.
5	If you feel like investing more time, that's fine.
6	Keep trying to be her friend.
7	Try harder.
8	Try harder and smarter.
9	Put making friends with this girl on the top of your list.
10	Really strive to be friends with her. Then you will thrive.

Now you know how to spot and "not" all the girls with low friendship ability. But enough about those four types of dead-end friends. You're interested in happy-ending friends. So on to that hot topic. How do you get to be friends with girls who are top friend material or could even turn into your best buds? Let's find out.

I felt so lonely, scared, and helpless before I found some friends. Now what a difference . . . Bianca, 17

Part II
Fab Friends

n., pl.: Solid, sound, and super chums

On to the hotter part of this book. So far you've learned which four types of girls to be wary of and watch out for. They're the kind of chicks that you want to nix being friends with. But don't worry. That's only about 25 percent at the max. In other words, it's only one-fourth of all the girls in your school and your life. Listen, if your school has 1,600 students, half will be girls, right? That's 800. And of the 800, one fourth is 200, which leaves three fourths and adds up to a whopping 600.

See what a huge number of friendly girls there are?

> What we did was include in our group some girls who were known to be mean. We kind of planned it. Took time, but now at our school, girl friends rule.
>
> Jessica, 17

Great work, Jessica! That's using your girl power for the good of everyone!

> Most of the girls at my school are cool. Once you talk to them, they're real friendly.
>
> Rose- Blue, 14

Good for you, Rose-Blue!

Yes, there are so many wonderful girls out there. They're independent minded like you and smart and spunky. They're girls who have so much to offer, girls on the go and grow, girls who are making a difference now or will soon. In short, terrific girls. Top chicks. And they come in all shapes and sizes and outer wrappings.

> The qualities I look for in a friend? None. I give every girl an equal opportunity to be my friend.
>
> Liza, 14

Liza has a great outlook. With all those opportunities you'll discover lots of fab friend material. That describes the greatest girls, girls you and everybody else likes and admires, not because they're perfect but because they are fun, focused on their futures, and self-reliant thinkers and doers. And most often up to something courageous or outrageous! And hilarious.

Or not.

> The friends I like know when to be serious. And when to freak!
>
> Jennifer, 17

Sure, generally friends are on the same wavelength, but not always. At times even your best friends can get on your last nerve, and you get on theirs. But that's just part of being friends—sometimes having a tiff or a little rift come between all of you.

> We like get into these huge fights but only now and then. And then we say sorry, and it's like when you break a bone. Once the fracture is healed, it's supposed to be stronger. Right? Same with our friendship.
>
> Diana, 14

That's right. With good friends, disagreements, even major ones, are never anything lasting because all of you together have so much going for yourselves, and you're always plotting and planning a meeting or going shopping or watching TV together.

> You got to be able to have fun together or else your friends will get very boring to you.
>
> Suzanne, 16

Three of my friends turned into my close friends. 'Cause they're honest and will listen to me even if they don't agree with everything I say. They're comforting and so nice.

Stephanie, 15

There's just something so special about the bonds of their friendship and so helpful and happy, yet also so cool and caring that their friendship's impact is life changing and lasting.

My friends have done me so much good. They stood by me when me and my family went through some hard struggles. Now everything's okay. No, it's ab fab (absolutely fabulous) because of my friends!

Annah, 18

If you don't have any great chick friends, and not even one best bud, you're missing out.

It takes a lot of courage to show your dreams to someone else. Erma Bombeck

Chapter 5
The Study Buddy

n., s.: A special chick; an academic, artistic, or tech chick; a mathematic, linguistic, poetic, scientific, scholastic, enthusiastic, athletic, energetic—you name it!—chick; an our-goals-just-click chick

What Makes a Girl a Study Buddy?

> The best way to find good friends is to take tough classes and get involved in all kinds of extracurricular activities.
>
> Nona, 15

How true. When you take challenging classes, plus participate in a sport or two, or get involved in a community club or a faith-based group, you will meet girls just like you—super girls with big goals. Girls who are busy being the best they can be and still have loads of fun.

> Don't be scared of checking out your different talents. That's when you can meet some real good friends.
>
> Jerry, 18

True. Developing the many abilities you have, or at least exploring them, should be part of your plan. And it's during that time that you can meet some of the dearest friends. Because what binds and bonds you is your common goal. And that's what a Study Buddy is—a plan pal or goal girl friend. So you want to have as many of them as you can snag. Because they're charging ahead just like you, and if you should waver, they can be a life saver and encourage you on.

> Dear Dr. Erika:
> I just started high school and it's like you wouldn't believe it. This superhuge school and this superhuge campus are like a college, you know? And I get lost, but that's not it. I get scared that I'm gonna mess up. The work is so much harder than in middle school, and the teachers go like they're on a tight schedule and have to catch a train that left ten minutes ago. And I worry all the time—so much that there's, like, this big knot in my stomach. But when I try to tell my friends about it, they blow me off. It's like they don't really care if they do bad in advanced biology.
>
> Vera, 14

FYI

Study Buddies are girls who are in your classes or academic clubs or groups and have the same drive you have, that is, to do well in school and to succeed. Or they may be on your soccer team or in your dance class.

But still they find a way, like you, to prioritize and know what's number one on their to-do list on a particular day. So that's the basis of your friendship with them—a common goal. If you have lots of Study Buddies, good for you! If not, like Vera, what a great chance to find some fast and then make those friendships last.

Just because you have a Study Buddy doesn't mean you sit around all day every day hitting the books! No way! Study Buddies do much more than that. In lots of ways, they're totally special friends.

Study Buddies aren't always the ones you see every day. More likely, they include a girl you run across during one of your extracurriculars. Or when you're volunteering at the nearby library, reading to the preschoolers during story hour.

Even if you can't see her every day, her friendship is a lot to be thankful for, and who knows, in the future, this friendship may develop even more. You might have to keep in touch via the Net for now, but once you can both drive, maybe you'll see each other more often. And waaaay off in the future, maybe you'll end up at the same college. If you keep in contact with the Study Buddy, the possibilities for a lifetime of friendship are endless!

Freedom High School, USA

The academic atmosphere at Freedom High is intense. After all, every year one or two students get a perfect SAT score. And this year it was three kids, juniors who got a 1600 on the SAT.

Wow. So Kim feels way nervous, especially today when she's being moved to an advanced math class. First thing this morning, her homeroom teacher gave her a new schedule. She did great on some state test, and this is her reward? Total bummer. Now Kim has to report to a new class in the third wing. The third wing is where all the prep courses are taught. And it's always a sea of seniors when you go down that hall. And they always glare at you like they know you're just a lowly soph wearing Target specials.

Kim dreads just thinking about fourth period. If she could only get sick and go home. But then what?

Kim wanders toward her new room and freezes outside her new classroom while a parade of preps rushes past. Many of them head for the new room too. Maybe they have a club meeting, or something, in there? So no chance approaching her new teacher quietly. Why is everything going wrong today?

"Come on in, Kim." A young teacher comes to the door, beckons her inside, then closes the door.

"How'd you know my name?" Kim asks timidly.

The teacher smiles. "I got a note and am glad to see you. Just make yourself at home, we'll talk later, all right?" She turns to a group of older girls. "Tone it down, please." The girls' voices drop noticeably as they pull their chairs together and go over some homework. Two of them walk to the chalkboard and start putting up bunches of numbers, then work a tough problem.

Everyone around her looks super busy, and Kim feels totally out of place. She sits down, trying to make herself small. Now her crazy stomach starts rumbling. How embarrassing! When a girl passes around a bag of chips, Kim's afraid to take some, even though she's starving. "You mean, you all get to eat in the classroom?" she whispers. "I thought the rule is—"

"Shh. Just be sure you don't leave any evidence, OK? The janitor sifts through the trash cans like a hotshot detective, and we don't want to get her in trouble." *Her* is the young teacher who's now at her desk munching away too.

Kim's hand sneaks into the depths of her backpack where she has an emergency energy bar and a small bottle of Evian tucked away. She feels guilty taking tiny bites, but as she does, she begins to relax. The trig-happy girls at the board are now on a problem that's caught her attention. She scoots closer to the front of the room, her eyes fastened on the calculations. But the girls go so fast that she can't understand what they're up to.

"What are they doing?" she asks another girl because she doesn't get it, all those fancy functions.

"I don't get it either, but I'm gonna copy it just in case . . . ."

Kim quickly stashes her trash in her backpack and follows suit. "Do you come in here every lunch?" she whispers.

"Yeah, sure, and it's done wonders for my report card."

Looks like Kim just found a Study Buddy, or several. What a relief. Now, how can you do the same?

FAST FRIENDSHIP FITNESS TEST

Could You Be a Study Buddy Repellent?

1 This year, you're in an honors English class. The class is challenging, but you're super excited about it. Sometimes you talk to the girl who sits next to you. Even though you've been in the same school since, like, the first grade, you've never really spoken to each other until

now—she always hangs with the "smart crowd." She asks if you'd like to get together after school and work on the homework. You:

a. Tell her you're busy. The truth is, you really want to hang out with her, but you're afraid to. See, she's really smart, and you're afraid that if you hang out with her, she'll think you're a silly klutz and that you can't do anything right.

b. Start memorizing the dictionary and pepper your speech with big words such as *asininity,* which you use to describe your brain-drained *former* friends.

c. Totally blow her off. Just because you're in one honors class doesn't mean you have to start hanging with the brain squad. Besides, you have your own group of friends and you're all really close—you don't need any more friends.

d. Are glad to have found another friend to add to your ever-increasing list. And what's so great with her is that she and you share a lot of goals. Even though you each have your own fab friends to hang with, you still enjoy getting together to study and hang out when you can.

2 **The gymnastics club you joined is filled with girls you'd like to talk to, but they've all been friends since kindergarten and you're new. You:**

a. Say a shy "Hi"—otherwise you're quiet and on a friendship diet. What's the use of trying to start a new friendship with them? They've got their own crew and they're probably not interested in hanging out with you.

b. Walk right up and act like you've known them forever. You laugh at all of their inside jokes, even when you don't get them, and you follow along wherever they go. You have a routine you've been working on that you'd like to show them, but in the end you chicken out and copy their routines instead. It's the kiss of death to stand out when you're the new girl on the team—better to go with the flow than get left out in the cold.

c. Show off your stellar skills like you're the next Carly Patterson. You may be the new girl in the group, but that doesn't mean you've got to hide in the corner. You're going to show them that you're the best. So what if they think you're a showoff? These girls aren't your friends—they're your competition. And you're playing to win!

d. Know in your heart that some of these girls could become your good friends, but you also know that it takes time to get to know someone, especially if they're already in a tight-knit group. So when the opportunity arises, you start talking and let the friendships develop. And they will!

3 Your mom tells you that the PTA just announced a statewide speech contest (with cash prizes!) and that several girls from other schools already signed up. Wouldn't it be nice if you entered too? You:

a. Say "No way!" What's Mom thinking? Your voice trembles when you read to your hamster. You would never have the guts to get up in front of the whole school and give a speech. They'd probably just laugh at you.

b. Talk to a couple of other girls who are entering and see what they're writing their speeches on and then you write yours on a similar subject. You're afraid that any idea you come up with on your own would get you laughed off the stage.

c. Check the list to see who else has entered. If you can see who your competition is, then maybe you'll enter—but only if you're the best person entering the contest!

d. Think about it carefully. It's your decision and you know it. You also know that you want to be a lawyer someday, or have some other awesome career. Maybe this is a good way to develop some super communication skills. You decide to go for it. A girl from your study hall is also entering the contest, so you practice reading your speeches to each other. No matter what the outcome, you had fun writing and practicing for it. And should you win, you'll get to buy that Banana Republic shirt you've been eyeing!

4 You signed up for a new science course this semester hoping to improve your grade. But all of the kids in your class are pretty laid back and just want to pass the class. You're disappointed because

you really wanted to learn and to pull your grade up. But there isn't anyone around that shares your views. You:

a. Feel like you should say something to the teacher about getting extra help, but you're afraid everyone will think you're a total nerd. So you stay quiet and suffer through it, even though the class could really hurt your GPA.
b. Try your best to get the work done, even if you don't understand it as well as you could. When you try and ask other girls in the class if they want to start a study group, they're not really interested—but they ask to copy your homework. You let them even though you're not sure you did it right. You'd rather join in than rock the boat.
c. Join in the goofing off and forget about trying to understand this science stuff. You'll probably never use it again anyway, so why bother making the effort. Better a bevy of bad-goal gals than no pals at all.
d. Ask to please be switched to a different class. If that's not possible, you get the e-mail addresses of some of the girls in the other class and try to Study Buddy with them. Over the Net, you bet. Just because your own class isn't into it doesn't mean you are going to stop learning and earning the grades you deserve.

Now it's time to find out your FQ: Tally your answers. How many A's, B's, C's, and D's do you have?

3 or 4 A's, check out Answer 1.
3 or 4 B's, check out Answer 2.
3 or 4 C's, check out Answer 3.
3 or 4 D's, check out Answer 4.

If you have a mixture of A's, B's, C's, and D's, look at all the answers. Obviously, there's a bit of everything in you, which is fab. Now, can you work on having a little less of the Answer 1 attitude and a little more of the Answer 4 attitude?

Answers

1 Skittish Kitty

You're so afraid of making a move and getting involved. Why are you so extra shy? Underneath your timid appearance lies a brave heart, remember, so make a start. Look up, speak up, and make yourself heard. In the process hook up with one or several new friends to study and learn with.

2 Sorry, Wrong Number

There's a defect in your connect. You want to find new friends, a few great study buddies among them, but your approach is all wrong. You seem to either read the potential friend pool incorrectly, or you dive in head-first but at the shallow end. Why don't you think a little more first and then act? Many good friends are out there just waiting for someone like you.

3 Ms. TKO

You've got a competitive streak a mile long! A little healthy competition is good, but why are you always trying to outdo everyone around you? You're a smart, motivated girl with a lot to offer, but if you keep trying to outshine everyone all the time, how are you going to form friendships that last? Hold on to your drive, but try to use it to help others out—not cancel them out!

4 Fun-tastic!

You enjoy meeting new people and trying new things—which makes it easy for you to find a great Study Buddy or two. That means, you and the rest of your independent-minded but studious pals have a grip on what's important during this time of your life—how to advance with the help of your many friends. Fantastic. And it's fun.

STUDY BUDDY FACTORS
What Should You Know about the Study Buddy?

Okay, so maybe studying isn't your fave thing in the world to do. But having a Study Buddy makes it so much better!

- ☑ Having a Study Buddy is like having a living and breathing study guide. It's like having a friend and a tutor all rolled into one.
- ☑ A good Study Buddy is a person who is motivated—just like you—to be the best she can be. So, by teaming with a Study Buddy, you're making the girl world—and your world—even stronger than it was before.
- ☑ A Study Buddy can get you motivated on even your most turned-off days when you dread reading up on another silly Punic War or way boring battle in your history book.
- ☑ And just think—on those crunch times when you have all of *The Great Gatsby* to review for your final, you can take the plot, one of your Study Buds can take the symbolism, and the other can bone up on the author info. And then you three share your knowledge. When you share the work, you end up with time to spare—meaning more time to do the fun things you want to do.

Goal and Study Buddies enable one another to reach for the stars and give one another a lift, a hoist up. Be grateful for their gift and return it manifold. Please.

FAST FRIEND MOVES
What You Should Do to Score a Study Buddy

1. Keep concentrating on your goals while looking to see if any other girls have the same idea. If they do, picture a whole pack of girls climbing up a mountain, okay? Goals are like mountains, so welcome the other girls' being by your side and ascending along with you.

2. Don't wait until you're doing bad in something or getting worse and worse. In every course and on every team, there's usually a girl (or two) who's better or more experienced or who's put in more effort. And that may even be you. So become friends with your teammates, club members, or fellow students and help them out, and they'll help you out.
3. Sometimes there's an atmosphere of stiff competition in sports and other extracurriculars. It's a wall that separates the girls from one another because each wants to do extra well and is only thinking of herself. But don't let that hold you back. Always give your advice freely. Show other girls the ropes. If possible, make the first move instead of always waiting for another girl to start the Goal/Study Buddy chain.

Whenever I'm new in a group, I say something to whomever is close by. Sometimes I say something dumb or goofy and that makes the other girls laugh at me. Sure, my face can turn beet red, but I always end up with a bunch of new friends.

Shannon, 16

FIRST PERSON

How I Handled It–Jamie's Real-Life Story

This new girl in my class, Jadah, looks scared a lot. When the bell rings and classes change, she always dashes out of the room and tries to beat the hall traffic. But she is super smart. When the teacher calls on her, she knows her stuff. Even when we're into tough new info, like logarithms, she always seems to know the answers!

Someone said this is her first year in public school. That she was homeschooled or whatever. The rumor is that she got bitten by a tick and got Lyme disease and that's why she couldn't come to school. So most people keep their distance.

Actually she's very unique and interesting. She has her own style that's really different from anyone else's in our school—but it's cool, you know? She mixes vintage stuff with hot new gear. She creates her own 'dos, also, like two ponytails on one side of her head, and next thing we know, the same design is showing up in, like, *CosmoGIRL!* Wow.

She sits by herself at lunch and eats the most unusual stuff, like yummy veggie sandwiches made by a deli. And she drinks crazy designer water with foreign labels. Last week my friends and me, we couldn't take it any longer. We got sooo curious about her. So we asked to sit with her and find out more. Turns out, Jadah hasn't had Lyme; she's been traveling with her 'rents. She's been to Kuwait, where she went to the American School, and everywhere else. So we've kind of become friends. And now we sit with her at lunch—she's so much fun. And in the process, we're, like, getting the inside scoop on the whole world. Plus we're catching on to logarithms. I guess you could call Jadah a Study Buddy and a friend all in one.—Jamie, 17

CHICK-POINT

Grade the Girls

F ✱
D ✱✱
C ✱✱✱
B ✱✱✱✱
A ✱✱✱✱✱

Chick Grades: ✱✱✱✱✱

Congratulations! Five stars to you, Jamie, and to your friends! You're one terrific group of girls. You didn't go the mean chick route and snub Jadah just because she's new or different. You guys acted mature—that's a sure meanness cure—and became Jadah's Study Buddies. Now you're learning from her and she from you. All girls have a lot to contribute, and who knows where this friendship will go? You may all end up making the honor roll and nabbing all kinds of top scholarships—because you banded together. One thing is certain, however: Your acting so friendly makes you a big success already!

Dear Diary

How many Study Buddies do you have in your life? Are you a good Study Buddy to those around you? By taking stock of yourself and knowing that you're a great girl with so much to offer, you can be a better friend to those around you. By now you know that the best Study Buddies for you are girls who have similar interests and goals. Still unsure of how to choose a Study Buddy who's right for you? Let's do a little exercise in your diary.

A-Plus Activities

In your diary, make a list of everything you're involved in during the course of a month. Don't leave anything out! Start with your school subjects, then go on to any sports or clubs you participate in. Then jot down any after-school lessons you take or part-time work you do or volunteer or faith-based activities you're a part of.

Next, write down your special abilities, your talents—even if nobody knows about them but you. Jot down your interests and dreams. Jot down the things you care about and the things you'd like to do in the future, even if you don't know how yet. And then the kinds of jobs you'd like to have later. And the one hot career you've always envisioned for yourself. What is it? Write it all down now.

Now think of the girls around you who are in similar classes or courses or activities—girls who may have similar talents or interests or heart's desires. Next, list their names and imagine at least one or two or three of them becoming your goal pals, your Study Buddies. Wouldn't that make everything so much easier?

And then know that you can make it happen. You—yes, you—can achieve your goals, and teaming up with a Study Buddy makes all of your dreams even more possible.

FRIEND SPOTTING
The Study Buddy

So now you know all kinds of great stuff about Study Buddies. If you already have a couple of these great girls on your side, good for you! But if you're still looking for a Study Buddy or two, some of the tips below might help you learn where to find her:

- ☑ Great Study Buddies can be found wherever girls go to study. That may be in your school's library or study center (if you have one). Or maybe you can find them in the local coffee shop or at the Barnes and Noble or Borders café.

At my school we have a little patio with picnic benches where girls go to study and stuff. So that's where I always go to find someone to help me with my geometry.

Jackie, 14

- ☑ Next time you're at softball practice or in class or in Girl Scouts or ballet, just look around at the other girls. They're all like you in some way; that's why they are there. So strike up a conversation with them—it could lead to wonderful things.
- ☑ School and extracurricular activities aren't the only ways to find a Study Buddy. There's always the Net or the phone. Goal pals don't have to meet face-to-face. They can interact with text messaging, e-mail, and even written notes. Where there's a will, there's a way.

At our first meeting, my club adviser let us exchange e-mail addresses. The rest is up to us and that's been so great. We're constantly back and forth with one another.

Liza, 14

Rx: Great Moves for Finding a Study Buddy

Know this for sure—a Study Buddy can cure any antistudy 'tude you may have. So scout one out. You can wait until others discover you, but what a drag it is to twiddle your thumbs and wait for fate. Why not make the first move? Whenever you come across a girl in any of your activities, just talk to her. Then, depending on her response, talk some more. And then talk to another girl. Before long, you will have a whole crew of girls with attitudes just like yours.

Chicks Mix

What's so great about Study Buddies is that making friends with them is easy. Since you're linked by a common bond—the goal to succeed and take the girl world by storm—you automatically have something in common. All you need to do is reach out to them, and you can find them anywhere! With the help of the Net, you can make Study Buddies all over the world!

Class Actions

If you're interested in what other girls from around the world are studying and thinking about, nothing can stop you from finding out. Ask your teacher to help you find some Study Buddies in Canada, Great Britain, South Africa, Australia, or New Zealand. Why from those countries? Because they speak English, so communication will be easier. Maybe you can even work to sponsor a class Study Buddy program in which your class e-mails students from other countries—kind of like having a pen pal. Most teachers or school librarians will know how to get you started, so don't be afraid to ask!

Chick-Mate

Study Buddies, and those include special buddies—girls whom you meet during one of your many outside activities—are the greatest of friends. They have great plans and super goals like you, and that's what gives your friendship substance. Flavor.

- Think about a few potential Study Buddies in your world.
- Next, mentally pick out one or two that seem approachable. And then approach them. Next time you see them, start talking to them and see if their hopes and plans match yours in some way.
- You can also go by Guidance and ask the counselor if he knows of another girl or two or three who are aiming high, like you do. Or check into the honor roll or dean's list bunch.

Whenever I meet a new girl at the Senior Center where I volunteer, I know we got lots in common. She wouldn't be there if she didn't care about making those grannies smile. And neither would I. So right away we're like buds.

Mally, 15

Friendship Finder

Overall, the Study Buddy is one of the greatest friends you can find, so go out and meet several of them. They rate a 7 or 8 or 9. Be sure to read the trusty Friendship Rating Scale to learn more.

FRIENDSHIP RATING SCALE

The Friendship Rating Scale goes from 1 to 10 (with 1 being way low and 10 being tops), which will help you make up your mind about which girls are hot friendship-wise and which for sure are not. You'll see a Friendship Rating at the end of each chapter!

1	Kick yourself for ever thinking about trying to be friends with her.
2	Serious waste of time.
3	May be a waste of time.
4	One more try can't hurt.
5	If you feel like investing more time, that's fine.
6	Keep trying to be her friend.
7	Try harder.
8	Try harder and smarter.
9	Put making friends with this girl on the top of your list.
10	Really strive to be friends with her. Then you will thrive.

Success . . . depends on your ability to make and keep friends. Sophie Tucker

Chapter 6

The Good Friend

n., s.: A true-and-tried chick, the cover-your-back and sympathetic chick, a unique chick with whom you just click

What Makes a Girl a Good Friend?

A Good Friend is a girl you're comfortable with and who makes your life more enjoyable. In other words, this is a girl who is a fab friend because she knows you and accepts you, as you do her, in equal measure. She is there for you when you're dolled up and looking like a million bucks, but also when you get drenched in a sudden downpour and resemble something the cat dragged in. She can laugh at the right moment or get you to laugh just when you need it most. In short, she's got the kind of personality that meshes with yours.

> The things that make up a good friend are personality, humor, and being able to stick by me, as I do them, through thick and thin.
>
> Ella, 14

Yes, good friends stick by you. They aren't perfect—none of us are—but they have so much friend potential that it's just so obvious. They make your everyday routines special. Even the most blah day becomes a great day because you have them. That's why you need to cultivate and cherish them.

Dear Dr. Erika:
Yesterday at a big recital I ran into a girl that I took ballet lessons with when I was in second grade. And man, she's so not changed one bit. Course she has on the outside. She's taller than me now and looks really good but is still sooo funny. She always made me laugh back then. So I started talking to her and right away she made me laugh again. It was cool, like time sorta melted away. Like we'd never been apart. But then she had to go back to the suburbs where she lives. Now I feel kinda empty.

Joanne, 15

FYI

Good Friends are friends who are just about perfect. Not that they're perfect in themselves, but you and they together are just about a perfect match. You can feel it. This is a real friendship, something solid, something lasting. That's what makes good friends so special—you are bonded with them in a unique way. And so, of course, you look forward to every time you get together with them, and they have the same feeling toward you.

This good friendship feeling can spring up overnight.

There's this girl I met last year. From the moment I talked to her, it was like talking to someone I'd known for years. Everything was just right.

Janis, 16

Good friendships don't always follow the same patterns. They can be as unique as snowflakes, as unique as the great chicks who make a Good Friend. But one thing is always true with Good Friends. You feel their presence in a positive way, and you feel a sense of loss in their absence.

And even if you don't have a Good Friend right now, you probably know a few girls who might just turn into your good friends. So for you, this chapter is even more important because it'll tell you how to transform a so-so friend into a superfriend—a fab friend.

In fact, good friendships are yours for the taking. Think of it this way: When you go shopping, there's all of this great stuff around you, right? And you get to pick and choose what you like. Well, think of your life like a huge friendship mall. There are all of these great girls all around you, and you get to pick and choose.

> Good Friends are girls I can get along with, and 'cause I'm easy to get along with, I can find good friends all over.
>
> Jane, 17

It's true. Good Friends can appear in so many places. And there are so many of them out there. That's why you need to know the four types of Good Friends.

"Now" Good Friends

First there are the *now* Good Friends. These are the Good Friends you have right now, at this very moment. Or a girl or girls whom you seem to be on the same wavelength with. Good Friends should be treasured—you are lucky to have them.

"Old" Good Friends

Next are the *old* Good Friends. These are the girls you've known a long time, like from kindergarten or first grade on, but maybe you don't live so close anymore or go to the same school. Like maybe they're from the old neighborhood you used to live in before Dad got transferred or Mom got downsized. Oh, those good old friends. They're the best in every aspect because they have proven their top friendship potential. They have, over the years, shared the highs and lows with you. They have been dreaming and scheming for fun along with you. And they still have everything you want in a Good Friend, except one important thing: physical closeness.

Boy Buds

Next are the Boy Buds. This is the boy you like but not like, *like* like. You like him because he's reliable and tells it like it is. You can do things with him that maybe your girl friends won't do—like outdoorsy kinds of stuff. In other words, he's a good guy pal, a funny and smart guy, a boy-next-door kinda bud.

> My guy friends are very dependable and honest. And for guys, they give the best advice ever.
>
> Tina, 18

True. Boy Buds are fabulous to have around because they are comfortable to be with and easy to talk to and fun to bum around with. And yet they can bring a different outlook to any chats you have with them.

> My Boy Buds are guys I can trust. I tell them anything and I know that they won't do anything to hurt me. And I never have to worry about them betraying me.
>
> Eileen, 15

So, having a Boy Bud, or two or three, is just great. You can learn a lot from them—about what makes boys in general tick and click. As for their friendship potential, it's there—in huge amounts.

"New" Good Friends

The last type of Good Friend is the *New* Good Friend. That's the girl or girls you have been distant friends with, or maybe it's a girl or girls you've never even talked much with, but you know—in your heart—that you could become good friends or even the best of friends. It's just a matter of time.

Freedom High School, USA

Haley hung around the mirror and the sink in the restroom, fussing with her hair and washing her hands for the tenth time, all the while waiting for the last girl to leave the stalls and get out of the bathroom. Finally, alone, aah! She found the cleanest spot on the floor. It was the one by the window that was painted over but still let in some light. She spread out her sweatshirt and sat down on the tiled floor. Flanked by her backpack on one side and her gym bag on the other, she leaned back against the wall and closed her eyes. She figured she could hang out here until she thought of a way out of this mess.

"Oh, here you are," came the cheerful voice of her new friend, Lindsey. "I've been looking all over for you. What's going on?"

"Nothing," Haley said, irritated, wondering how she could get rid of Lindsey. She liked Lindsey a lot, but she just needed some time alone to think. "I'm just on my way to practice and I stopped here to . . . change my shoes. I gotta run."

Lindsey looked satisfied with Haley's answer. "Okay, bye, but are we still eating at your house? Your Mom said to tell you she's fixing your favorite din-din. To celebrate your report card."

Haley groaned. "Oh no, oh no! That's why I'm in here, hiding in this stinky bathroom! I don't have practice today. I'm hiding because I got a C-minus!"

Lindsey crossed over and hunched down. "Oh, I'm sorry, I had no idea."

"Well, yeah, neither did I. But last week when we had this away match, I missed a test. And then I, like, totally forgot about making it up."

"Well, don't worry, your mom will understand. She's cool and stuff like that can happen to anybody. Just explain it and then take the makeup—"

Haley groaned again and cut Lindsey off. "You don't get it, do you? The time for makeups is over. Old Ms. Prune left a message on our machine to remind me to come in early last Friday."

"Why didn't you?"

"'Cause I was scared out of my mind Mom would find out. So I erased the message and then I overslept and then . . . oh, I don't know. It all kind of snowballed and now I can't go home. Mom will just kill me. . . ."

"Maybe it isn't too late," Lindsey mused, then went on. "You know what? I think Ms. Prune's still in the chemistry lab. So, maybe if you explain to her what happened? Maybe if you tell her you're real sorry and that you won't mess up again? Anyway, she's always the last to leave. So why don't we—"

"Uh-uh. No way. I can't face her. She's gonna give me a long lecture and stuff."

"Well, can't be that bad, really. I'll wait in the hall for you, okay? I totally know how you feel because I went through something like this last year. But trust me, you'll feel a lot better if you figure it out. It will only get worse if you ignore it. Trust me! When you're done in there, let's go and grab something to eat and put this bad day out of our minds!"

> *My good friends are always there when I need help. Plus, they help me through whatever, every time. I don't know what I'd do without them.*
>
> *Kerrie, 17*

So, it's clear. You need one or several Good Friends—ASAP, right? But how do you get them?

FAST FRIENDSHIP FITNESS TEST

Are You a Good Friend?

1 A close friend of yours has suddenly started withdrawing from you. Now she's hanging out with a group of girls with a really bad reputation—girls she never even used to talk to. She's totally giving you the cold shoulder. You:

a. Watch sadly and from a distance, dreaming of the good old days in sixth grade when you and your friend dressed in matching outfits and ate blue Jell-O, which nobody else liked. Alas, alas, that time has passed.

b. Slip her a note that says, "When you play with fire, you can get burned." Then you scoot along, wondering how long it will take your friend to figure out what you mean. The trouble chicks she's chilling with are the fire, of course. Will your friend catch on to the meaning before she gets suspended right along with her new crew?
c. Join in with your friend and her new mean chick crowd, even though it's not exactly your style. Maybe if you think up newer and even worse rule-breakers every day, they'll rally round you. Then your friend will come a-running fast, back into your innermost circle.
d. Tell her it's time for a heart-to-heart. Be frank and inform her of what you know about that bunch of mean queens. Point out that spending lots of time around a negative influence can make you negative. Keep talking to her about this and don't give up. Good friends are priceless, you know? And you're a charge taker, not a friend forsaker.

2 An old friend you haven't seen in years suddenly e-mails you. You:

a. Smile, get out your old scrapbook that has pictures of the two of you having so much fun. Even that one time when you swore you'd always be friends. You shed a tear and dab it away with a pink tissue. Life is sooo sad.
b. E-mail back right away, with thanks. "Nice hearing from you," you write, and attach a flowery border. Then mark her off your to-do list. You like to always get everything done as soon as possible, especially your correspondence. There, all finished.
c. Call her, e-mail her, and instant message her every day. Wow, finally, here's your chance to catch up. You send her copies of your best jokes and dish all the gossip that's been going around. You FedEx her a collection of toy pigs—she used to love them—then wonder why she doesn't respond in kind. What a bad friend she is!
d. Send her a brief e-mail telling her you're glad to hear from her. You ask her a few questions and fill her in on what's

been happening with you. But only a couple of highlights. You include your phone number and tell her you hope to hear from her again. You'd love to keep in touch with her—she's a great girl. But the next move is hers.

3 A teacher in your school is going on maternity leave, which means two classes will be combined. That means your longtime Boy Bud is now in the same room with you. The first day you have class together, he snags a seat across the room and waves at you. You:

a. Pretend you've never seen him before and, your face flaming up, retreat to the coat closet. Oh no, hope nobody noticed him looking at you—you don't feel like getting teased.

b. Wave shyly, then get back to work. Later when you get a moment, you write him a note asking him to not let anyone know that he knows you. See, somebody might actually come to the wrong conclusion about you two, and that's what you do not want.

c. Flirt outrageously and victoriously with him and let the other girls know he's yours, and yours alone! Any girl giving him the eye will hear from you! And it won't be pretty.

d. Treat him like the good friend he's always been. You introduce him around to your friends in class and explain the ins and outs to him, as time permits. Sure is nice to have another bud around, especially in this class, which can be a pain.

4 A new girl transfers from another school and joins your tennis team. She looks really nice, but it's her first day and she's standing by herself. You:

a. Look at her when she's not looking and wish, wish, wish she would be your friend. That would be so nice, to have somebody to whisper with now and then, here and there. Maybe some day. For the time being, you just look.

b. Say hi to the new girl and talk to her throughout the whole practice to let everyone know that she's your new friend. Within minutes of meeting her, you invite her over after school and to sleep over at your house this coming weekend, forgetting that you've already made plans with your best girl buds to hang out. If you really hate her after spending time with her, you'll just go back to your old friends. Then nobody can say you didn't try.

c. Are so sick and tired of all kinds of girls trying to horn in on your act. You can tell by the way she's standing there that she thinks she's Little Miss Tennis Star. Well, there's only room for one star on the team, and that star is you! You make sure to leave her out of your circle of friends on the team, and you shoot her icy stares whenever you get the chance. You'll show her who's boss!

d. Are glad that there's a new member on your team. And this girl seems to have a great backhand, so, of course, you compliment her on it. Next thing you know, you're talking about the tennis stars both of you admire. In a week, there will be an exhibition match close by, with a former Wimbledon player. Maybe you'll see her there. Won't hurt to ask her about it.

Now it's time to find out your FQ: Tally your answers. How many A's, B's, C's, and D's do you have?

3 or 4 A's, check out Answer 1.
3 or 4 B's, check out Answer 2.
3 or 4 C's, check out Answer 3.
3 or 4 D's, check out Answer 4.

If you have a mixture of A's, B's, C's, and D's, look at all the answers. Obviously, there's a bit of everything in you, which is fab. Now, can you work on having a little less of the Answer 1 attitude and a little more of the Answer 4 attitude?

Answers

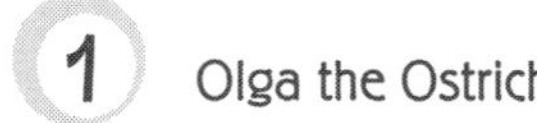

1 Olga the Ostrich

Being invisible doesn't make you invincible. So take a deep breath and get into the game—of life. Oh sure, that doesn't mean everything's always going to be just peachy. You will have to deal with some unpleasant things now and then, but at least you're alive. Think of all of the great friend opportunities you're missing out on by hiding out all the time! Next time, try taking a chance—you'll be pleasantly surprised by where it may lead!

2 Hesitating Essie

You're on the right track, girl. That means you try to be a Good Friend, but building a good friendship takes lots of time and effort. You can't just turn it on and off like a switch! In order to have a Good Friend, you have to prove you're a Good Friend yourself. And Good Friends are there for each other, even if it takes a little effort.

3 Fighting Fiona

You're a girl with a lot going for yourself. Unfortunately, you're in constant conflict with other girls to such a degree that whatever good is in you doesn't have a chance to shine. Why don't you exhale, then get a personality makeover? You can't expect to make Good Friends who stick by you if you're competing with them all of the time.

4 Fab Friend

Yes! Good work! You have the self-confidence to attract Good Friends and keep them. That's because you are such a Good Friend yourself. And how lucky your pals are to get to be around you. They know they can count on you and your good and independent judgment—not to mention your smarts and your big heart.

GOOD FRIEND FACTORS

What Should You Know about the Good Friend?

Good Friends are a necessity, really. You need them to live your life with smarts and style—no doubt about it.

- ☑ Good Friends make your life better! Without them, you would trudge through your days with all sorts of stuff weighing you down because you don't have anyone to talk to.
- ☑ Good Friends are good listeners—they'll always take the time to listen if you're having a problem or a bad day.
- ☑ You can have a wide circle of Good Friends, or maybe just one or two close friends. No matter how many you have, make sure to be as good a friend to them as they are to you!
- ☑ The Good Friends you make now will be with your forever!

FAST FRIEND MOVES

What You Should Do to Score a Good Friend

1. Think about all your friends. You may have one or two Good Friends with whom you're super close. Or you may have more Good Friends than you can count on your two hands. Either way, you're doing great! There are always ways to add to your friend collection, and as you grow and change, your friendships will too.

   Moving when you're in high school ranks with the worst nightmares you can have. I know, my dad's in the Army. So every time I have a bunch of good friends, I'm out of here—off to another base or place, whatever. But then I realize this is just another terrific opportunity to make a brand-new bunch of pals.

   Morgan, 13

2. You can also add to your friend collection by getting closer to the girls you already know from a distance or by re-establishing bonds with former good friends.

It's tough to have a good friendship with a girl who lives in Dallas, once you move to Detroit. But it can be done and it's so much fun. E-friends are e-xcellent.

Tasmin, 14

3. Be willing to accept a few Boy Buds into your group. In other words, expand your narrow circle into a real wide one, and then reinforce that friendship field by acting friendly every day.

Good friends are nice to each other, and talk and laugh together whenever they get a chance.

Shauna, 16

4. Finally, scout about for brand-new friends. That means you don't close your circle when new girls appear on the horizon. Think about it—if you hunker down with one or two close pals and don't open yourself up to meeting new people, you're missing out on tons of chances for more friends—and more fun. So always be willing to meet and make new friends. Each new friend can contribute so much to your life.

I'm always on the lookout for more good friends. They're like money in the bank to me. The more friends I've got, the more the interest adds up—in my life. Yay.

Kori, 18

FIRST PERSON

How I Handled It-Coco's Real-Life Story

My ninth-grade prom totally ruined me. What it was, there was this tenth-grade boy who asked me to the prom and I couldn't believe it. I was so excited! All of my other friends went stag in a group, and I was the only one with a real date. Even a limo came by. The boy's parents were, like, so rich, and I'd spent weeks agonizing over every detail. I had my dress made by my nana. Lime green lace and tulle and spaghetti straps and stuff, and new shoes—this high. Actually I had to learn to walk in them. And my hair was done by a stylist who once used to do the hair of Laurie Dhew, that news announcer on TV, you know?

It was a huge day. All my friends came and helped me. I mean they did my makeup, glittery eye shadow and all. It was like a group project except the project was me. My friends were so sweet; they spent hours fixing me up.

You know what? The first thing when we got to the prom, the boy dumped me. Turned out, his parents had forbidden him to date this other girl. He wasn't allowed to even look at her, so he picked me because I was a nobody. Once we got to the prom, he ditched me for her. He used me! It was awful, but my friends were there and they made me feel sooooo much better. They tried to make me laugh and we danced all night to our favorite songs. I can't imagine what it would have been like if my friends hadn't been there for me. They helped to make the worst night into one of the best nights ever!

But now there's another thing. This other boy I've known for years asked me to go with him to a movie with a bunch of other boys and girls, like in a group. Just as friends. But my girl friends all go, "Don't even think about it." When I told them he's a long-time bud and I enjoy talking to him, they said, "Forget it. Don't you remember what happened at the prom?"

But this is different. This boy isn't that type. He isn't going to just use me. We just like to hang out. But the girls say I have to choose—between being their friend and his friend. They want me to snub every guy just because of what happened at the prom.

I thought about it long and hard. Then I made up my mind and told them that I'm not choosing. I'm going to be friends with them and with him.—Coco, 15

Chick Grades: ✱✱✱✱✱

Good job, Coco! You deserve the highest grade: five stars with bells and whistles and all kinds of plusses. Never choose between good friends. Keep being their good friend, and if that doesn't suit some of them, then that's *their* problem. They're just out of luck because your friendship is special, precious, and true-blue. And if they want to miss out on it, then that's their mistake.

CHICK-POINT

Grade the Girls

F *

D **

C ***

B ****

A *****

Dear Diary

It's diary time again! Get out your trusty diary and take out four clean sheets of paper. Head the first one "Now Friends," the second one "Old Friends," the third one "Boy Buds," and the last one "New Friends."

Then write the numbers 1 to 10 on each page and fill in the names of all your friends according to what category they fall under.

If you can fill in a name after each number, congrats to you! But if you have mainly blank spaces or almost all blanks, double congrats to you! Now you have the chance to meet all kinds of new friends and add their names as you do. And this friend-making process is going to be one of the greatest things you've ever done. So, to get you all psyched up, turn over the lists now and write down how you think you could possibly meet these new good friends and all the places where you think you might meet them. Then look at the friend-friendly advice below and compare your answers.

FRIEND SPOTTING

The Good Friend

The Good Friend is way essential. You need her to really get everything out of your life that you can—not just the credits for schoolwork done and the trophies for excelling on the swim team, but the pure enjoyment of good times. Fun is so much more fun when it's shared with someone.

And you'll need a Good Friend to make it through the bad times, the sad times with. Good Friends can up any downs ASAP.

- ☑ You can find Good Friends anywhere—in your classes, on your team, in your clubs, and during all those activities that keep you hopping.

  What I do is make a suggestion to my crew, like, Anyone want to go to the mall Saturday? There's always a few who do. That's all it takes to get a good friendship started—spending time with girls who are fun.

  Bella, 15

- ☑ You can even find Good Friends on the Net. You can chat with girls you already know, or you can e-mail old friends with whom you've lost contact. Now is a good time to re-establish that connection.
- ☑ You can add to your Boy Bud list by not freaking out any time a boy says hi to you. Just say hi back and talk to him—a little. But don't jump to the conclusion that he's the guy of your dreams!

  Just be friendly, but not flirty, to the boys in your circle.

  Amber, 16

  In my Life Science class there is this shy boy who always moves his desk next to mine when the teacher says it's group work. He's real smart and knows all about the labs and stuff, but the other girls tease me and call him my puppy dog!

  Angie, 14

  Boy Buds have feelings too, you know.

  Peter, 15

Rx: Great Moves for Finding Good Friends

To find Good Friends, you just have to take a good look around, because they can be found in many, many places.

1. Open your eyes and put a friendly expression on your face at all times. Down with the frown.

   You can find good friends in the same class, riding the same bus, walking down the hall, or at the movies while waiting in line.

   Adria, 16

2. Don't expect Good Friends just to show up suddenly on your doorstep. You have to be an active participant in life and be willing to be involved in various things, not just doing the same old, same old every day, like just going to school, then home, then hiding in your room, and once in a while going to the store.

   Because I want lots of good friends, I can't just find them at the grocery store in the Pepsi aisle.

   Yoanna, 17

3. Increase the number of your activities, in school and out, and your chances of connecting with lots of good friends will shoot sky high. And once you see some girls who look like they might be Good Friend matches, start up a conversation with them.

Chicks Mix

Want to make new friends but feeling a little shy? No worries! It's totally normal to feel a little nervous when you're meeting new friends. There are lots of different ways to meet people. Check out some of these super simple ways to approach a new friend.

First you greet the person with a smile and a "hi" or "hey"—whatever form of greeting is most common in your area. Next, start talking about something lightweight—such as the weather, the class, the corn dogs at lunch, the crowds, the noise—whatever is happening around you that's obvious to everyone. Any opening comment will do, as long as it's light. Think soup and salad rather than a full-course meal, conversationwise.

Finally, and this is key, say something nice and complimentary about the new girl you're trying to become friends with. Say something about how you like what she said in class today or how you wish you had shoes like hers. Or mention something cool you have noticed about her. But don't go into anything personal or negative.

> Under no circumstances comment on her onion breath after she just ate that hot dog with everything if you're trying to make a new friend!
>
> Gena, 16

True, so keep your first chat chatty, friendly, and open-ended.

In the next chapter, you'll learn all about making that new friendship that you're trying to build stronger, deeper, more meaningful—and lasting.

Chick-Mate

Overall then, the Good Friend is the greatest and fabbest of friends. You and all your Good Friends together will have such a blast, even when things get tough. And they do, sometimes, in everyone's life! You know that. For that reason, the more Good Friends you have, the better for you. Each one will help you in some small or large way. Each one will make your life easier or more fun.

> The good friends I'm always on the lookout for have a super personality, a sense of humor, and are outgoing, smart (I mean, they have common sense plus care about their education), helpful, and most of all they act like real friends. And with their help, I feel like I can achieve anything.
>
> La Monica, 16

Yes, La Monica, you can achieve anything you want with the help of your good friends, and they can, too, with your help. So here's the deal:

> Old friends have a very high friendship potential but only if you get it and get busy reconnecting. Takes a little bit of effort—but what a reward.
>
> Steph, 18

Don't forget to invite a few Boy Buds into your crowd. Most important of all, go out and meet several *new* best friends. Start today and keep it up. Your future Good Friends are waiting for you right now! This minute. All you have to do is be willing to meet them.

FRIENDSHIP RATING SCALE

The Friendship Rating Scale goes from 1 to 10 (with 1 being way low and 10 being tops), which will help you make up your mind about which girls are hot friendship-wise and which for sure are not. You'll see a Friendship Rating at the end of each chapter!

Friendship Finder

Good Friends rate a 9 or 10. As always, you make the final decision, so consult the Friendship Rating Scale for details.

1	Kick yourself for ever thinking about trying to be friends with her.
2	Serious waste of time.
3	May be a waste of time.
4	One more try can't hurt.
5	If you feel like investing more time, that's fine.
6	Keep trying to be her friend.
7	Try harder.
8	Try harder and smarter.
9	Put making friends with this girl on the top of your list.
10	Really strive to be friends with her. Then you will thrive.

Part III
Best Buds

n., pl.: Top-pick and up-tick chicks

And now to the hottest and best part of this book—wow. We're talking about what and who are closest to your heart. What really, really matters. And that's finding at least *one* girl, or two or three, to always be there for you. To be your Best Bud.

Best Buds have top friendship talent and that's quite obvious in the way they treat you.

> My Best Buds and I are able to confide in one another and talk about everything. Really, truly.
>
> Nicola, 16

And what a comfy feeling this is—to have one or two or even three girls who you can dish with about every topic in the world.

> Even on a nasty rotten yuck day, when I meet up with my Best Buds, the sun breaks through.
>
> Alicia, 15

True. Best Buds do have that incredible ability to make an ugly day better and to make your life better. All is takes is one Best Bud, but there's no rule that says you can't have more than one. Or two or three or more.

> There's four of us that are, like, quads. We're always together and getting into silly jams but we also get out of them fast 'cause we are Best Buds.
>
> Jaylee, 14

So, how can you start having at least one Best Bud? Maybe even two or three?

Sometimes it seems like it just happens. One girl in your world stands out and she's the one you run to in case of a crisis or a huge celebratory moment.

My Best Buds and I just found each other, you know?

Scarlett, 15

That's so wonderful—that finding each other. But what Scarlett didn't say is that she was *open* to finding some Best Buds, that she positioned herself to find some, and that her attitude and actions were the *real* reasons she nabbed those Best Buds. It was her own increased friend potential—in this case, her own increased Best Bud potential—that caused those other girls to choose her as their Best Bud in return!

In other words, it really wasn't anything that just happened.

Scarlett empowered herself. She made it happen.

Just like you will, starting right now.

Oh, the comfort, the inexpressible comfort of feeling safe with a person, having neither to weigh thoughts nor measure words. Dinah M. Mulock Craik

Chapter 7
The Best Bud

n., s.: A very close, solid-as-a-brick chick; a tickles-me and sticks-up-for-me chick; a fantastic, dynamic, and going-places chick—just like yourself

What Makes a Girl a Best Bud?

> *A Best Bud is a girl who will be there for you through the end of time, at least through high school and college. Through all the good and the bad.*
>
> Nini, 17

She's waiting for you when you get to school, and you know where because she left you a message. And when she's late, you know why and aren't worried. You know that during morning break she'll fill you in on what you've missed out on. Or between classes. And if that doesn't work, she'll e-mail you later with the latest details.

And you, having kept her in mind meanwhile, will fill her in too, so both of you will always be in the know. For sure. And when something's going on around you, you make a mental note to tell her later, and you do. And she'll do the same for you.

> *My best bud is Joie. She likes everything I like, talking, going to the mall, discussing other girls and guys. We do stuff like this all the time and often end up in funny situations.*
>
> Amira, 15

Then the two of you laugh about it, right? That's what Best Buds are for.

Best Buds also make embarrassing moments less I-could-just-die! moments.

> My Best Buds give me lots of courage and confidence 'cause even if the worst comes to pass and my period soaks through my white skirt!—they will not turn their backs on me.
>
> Kenyatta, 16

> Dear Dr. Erika:
> This happened when I had to move. It was when I was going into the seventh grade. My family and I left upstate New York to move down here. This was devastating to me. I had to leave everything behind that I had established in my life. Although it wasn't that much, it still meant the world to me. My best friend was Jillie—it was really hard saying good-bye to her. Even though we swore we'd always be friends, we only exchanged a few letters and then we kind of stopped writing.
>
> But guess what? When I went to band camp last week, guess who was there? Jillie. She had moved too and now lives only fifteen minutes away. She rushed over as soon as she saw me, and it was just like old times, but even better. I can tell her everything and I did.
>
> And do. Every chance I get. Wow. She's my Best Bud.
>
> Erin, 15

FYI

Best Buds are the dearest and closest friends you can have. They know you well, like you lots, even with your little quirks and even if you're in a really bad mood. They feel the same way about many things as you do. They laugh with you, cry with you, and share what's inside them.

Some girls call their Best Bud their twin sister, but not by accident of birth, by choice. Why? Because if out of all the girls in the world you could pick the one who's an ultrabest friendship match for you, then this is the one, the girl you can come to anytime—day or night—even at midnight. You could—without disturbing her family, of course—wake her up and tell her everything, and I mean everything.

Yes, your Best Bud is truly a great chick who will always support you, always encourage you, always cheer you up, always listen to you, always fight for you, and even give you her last dime. She's that good a bud.

And, of course, Best Buds require that you treat them the same. A Best Bud relationship is always a two-way street. If it's one-sided, it's going to flop. So having a Best Bud means being a Best Bud.

> I let my Best Buds use all my best stuff 'cause I know they'll give it back, even dry-cleaned! Even with a loose button sewn on. Whatever.
>
> Caroline, 16

Best Buds don't share just their possessions, they share their time. They drop everything, rush over to your house, and spend time with you. They'd go through the fire for you—and you for them. Honest. And they are at their most steadfast and dependable in a major crisis.

Freedom High School, USA

Ann didn't know how it started—that awful nervous feeling she had all the time, 24/7. Maybe it was when her teachers suddenly piled on too much homework while she was trying out for cheerleading, which was way rough. Or maybe it was when the cheer uniform her sisters had worn didn't seem to fit her anymore. Ann hadn't pigged out, but still she seemed to gain a bunch of weight overnight. It was like a sausage roll took up residence around her middle and wouldn't leave.

Or maybe it was when Ann overheard her parents fuss a lot and talk about getting a divorce. Then Nana got really sick and had to go to the hospital. So it was just like stress after stress coming down on her like a constant downpour until Ann thought she couldn't take it anymore. Oh, how she dreaded going to school every morning, especially now that her Best Bud, Tawanna, was off in Washington, D.C., on some sort of Young Pols powwow. For a whole week, too!

Anyway, Ann dreaded going home in the afternoons even worse.

So, she started doing it to release some of her stress. Yanked at her bangs, which always got in her way when she was trying to read. Or got in her eyes when she fretted about her sucky life. So she plucked at her hair, first at the hairline, just a tug. It hurt but felt good because it focused all her worries on this one thing—the hair pulling. Anyway, nobody knew what she was doing because she just pulled her hair down over where she had pulled some out.

First she did just her bangs. Then she started in on the back of her head. Each time she pulled out a hair, it felt like she was getting some control back over her life. Sort of like a hair yanked out made a little hole to release all that stress building up in her. Really it was no big deal. It was her hair and she did it only when she was by herself. So, who cared?

Tawanna did.

On Thursday of the week she was supposed to be in D.C., when Ann thought she was alone in a study carrel at the school library, Tawanna came striding in, her hands propped on her hips. "What's going on?" she demanded.

"Nothing, except the usual junk," Ann said, quickly finger-combing her hair over all the places she had plucked. "And, um, what about you? Aren't you supposed to be gone until—"

"Most of the meetings I cared about were over this morning. So I talked Dad into picking me up early and running me by here."

"Why?"

"Because I'm worried about you."

Ann swallowed and quickly put her notebook on top of the dozens of long hairs she'd pulled out. "Why?"

"'Cause you sounded so stressed out every time I called you from D.C., and now I see . . ."

"See what?"

"This," Tawanna said, pointing. "Look." She dug out a small mirror, held it up, and swept back the bangs from Ann's forehead, revealing a bald patch. Then she pulled a chair over, sat down, and said, "Want to talk about it?"

"No," Ann said. Admitting that she'd been yanking out her hair just to feel the tiny stabs of pain so she wouldn't have to think about all the big pains in her life sounded crazy. And she wasn't crazy! "It's nothing, just something to do when I'm bored."

"Yeah, right." Tawanna put her arm around Ann. "C'mon." She marched Ann straight to the Guidance Department and waited with her until a counselor was free. Then she told Mrs. Taylor what she had seen Ann do. And then she left.

But from then on, Ann had someone to talk to; not only Mrs. Taylor, who had her come in once a week, but also Tawanna. And she found out what she had, a disorder called trichotillomania. Trich, for short. That means, compulsive hair pulling.

And she felt much, much better. Mrs. Taylor said it was stress related, after Ann spilled everything, all her worries, fears, and frustrations. Which was good because she got help dealing with everything. She got a lighter schedule and balanced out her honors classes, and Mrs. Taylor talked to her parents. In no time Ann felt hopeful again, which she hadn't for a long time. Nana got better, too.

Best of all was knowing she had a Best Bud who really cared and made sure she got the help she needed. Yeah, Tawanna was a rock. There for Ann during their junior year and for years to come. They even talked about being in each other's wedding someday.

• • •

So, what can you do to find your own Best Bud or Buds? How can you become part of such a close and wonderful friendship?

First off, let's make sure you're not a Best Bud blocker. That means that you don't, consciously or subconsciously, do something to keep your Best Buds away from you.

FAST FRIENDSHIP FITNESS TEST

Are You a Best Bud?

1 Your Best Bud gets an entirely different schedule from yours and won't be in any of the same classes or clubs as you. And you have late lunch but she has early lunch. Up to now you've been practically twins. Now what? You:

a. Creep along during your day, feeling blue that you've lost your best friend. You wonder if you'll ever find another Best Bud again.

b. Write her long and flowery letters and e-mails, reminiscing about the good old days when you were together all of the time. You include a snapshot of you two going down a water slide together during a long-ago field trip, just so she won't forget her former Best Bud—you.

c. Stalk into the main office, flanked by two high-priced lawyers, and scream about discrimination and folks always being out to get you. You promise a big lawsuit. How dare these school fools stick you with a schedule that separates you from your Best Bud? You'll take this all the way to the Supreme Court!

d. Make some terrific plans with her. Monday evening you'll call her. Tuesday, she'll call you. Wednesday you'll get together at the community youth group—something new for both of you. And so on. That's in addition to the usual text and instant messaging. Actually, this is going to work out fab because now you both have new worlds to conquer. Then you can share your new adventures. And think of all the weekends, holidays, and other days off you can spend together. Absence makes a Best Bud's heart beat faster because she soaks up what's happening separately, then has more to tell.

2 Your Best Bud starts spending a lot of time with a new girl who just enrolled in your school. She keeps telling you that you're still her best friend, but she doesn't act like it. Every time you look, they have their heads together and they are giggling. You:

a. Slink away to the nearest bathroom, where you examine yourself inch by inch. No wonder they're giggling, you decide. Your bangs are lame. Your outfit sucks. If it weren't all so sad, you'd giggle too.

b. Think of course your Best Bud prefers spending time with the new girl. She's smarter, funnier, has a better personality, and looks a little like Jessica Simpson. How can you compete with that? I mean, c'mon. Better just forget it.

c. Sashay right up to your former Best Bud and confront her. Words that are usually found on the walls of public restrooms erupt from your mouth like you are Mount Vesuvius. You're not going to take it from this traitor, and you make sure everybody knows it, too.

d. Join your Best Bud and the new girl and ask what's so funny. If they're glad to see you and clue you in, giggle along with them. Later you talk with your Best Bud and explain that her focus on the new girl is making you feel bad. If she's truly your Best Bud, she'll see the error of her ways and things will work themselves out for the best.

3 Your Best Bud is beginning to mess up seriously. Suddenly she's letting stuff she used to care about slide and she's starting to hang with girls that are known mean chicks. And she constantly talks about sneaking out and going to parties and smoking and drinking. She was never like this at all before! You:

a. Shake your head at the change that's come over your Best Bud and scurry away to your next class. You don't want to get involved in that kind of stuff. Maybe if you stop overhearing what your Best Bud's talking about, she'll snap out of it.

b. Leave her anonymous notes here and there about the wild child she's about to turn into. You also sneak a pamphlet about the dangers of bad habits into her book bag. And you give the mean chicks a furtive glare. You hope that sooner or later your Best Bud gets the message.

c. Can't wait until your parents go to their next out-of-town meeting. You'll tell them you're going to sleep over at your

Best Bud's house. What's one little fib? And she'll do the same. Then you have a blast for the whole weekend long. Wow. And she can invite all her super new friends, too.

d. Have a talk with her—openly and honestly—about what you have observed with your own eyes. And you back up your talk with facts, and prove to her how her actions are beginning to affect her work. You tell her that you care for her and will do anything to help her. If she'll listen to you, good for you! And her! If she doesn't, you'll enlist the help of someone in authority. Sometimes being Best Buds requires getting each other back on track.

4 You're really concerned about your Best Bud. All of a sudden, she's too busy to talk to you and hang out with you. She's always sitting by the phone, waiting for her new guy to call. Neither one of you has ever really had a boyfriend before and you definitely feel kind of left out. You:

a. Know there's nothing you can do. You're no match for a cute boy, so you just stay out of her way. You silently wish them well—maybe you'll be invited to the wedding.

b. Get out your mom's palette of eye shadows, liners, blushes, and brushes. If your Best Bud has found a guy, you'll help her cement their relationship. Fast. So you give her an extreme makeover to help her look her best. And you're super nice to her so she doesn't forget about you. Who knows? Maybe her guy has a friend he'll send your way.

c. Become Ms. Male Magnet. This is war, okay? If your Best Bud can attract a wimpy little stud, then you can become the Paris Hilton of the Polo Team. You step into the highest stilettos and the skimpiest skirt and you flirt like you've never flirted before. If she wants to tie herself down to one guy, you'll make sure you have a whole army of guys chasing you!

d. Realize that your Best Bud has a boyfriend, and you're glad for her. But that's not going to come between you, 'cause you won't let it. So, you'll keep on being her best

> friend and hope she'll do the same. Meanwhile, you have other friends, and when your Best Bud is busy with her beau, you just spend time with the rest of the crew. Hanging your head over your Best Bud's boyfriend is so not you. Sure, you'll tell her you miss her when she's busy with him, but you have too much to do, too much to get done. Hey, you're on your way—as always.

Now it's time to find out your FQ: Tally your answers. How many A's, B's, C's, and D's do you have?

3 or 4 A's, check out Answer 1.
3 or 4 B's, check out Answer 2.
3 or 4 C's, check out Answer 3.
3 or 4 D's, check out Answer 4.

If you have a mixture of A's, B's, C's, and D's, look at all the answers. Obviously, there's a bit of everything in you, which is fab. Now, can you work on having a little less of the Answer 1 attitude and a little more of the Answer 4 attitude?

Answers

Timid Kimmie

Having a Best Bud is wonderful. You have to realize that and stop being such a quiet little mouse. When something, or someone, threatens your ties, look them in the eye and face the threat. When you retreat timidly every time, you're giving in to defeat—without even trying.

Show-off Suzie

You think you're showing your special friendship with your Best Bud, but most of your efforts are just for show. Or they're totally misdirected. So stop acting like a seesaw and stick out your jaw a little. You can take a strong stand without offending others. Do it. Speak up.

3 Pitbull Penelope

Biting or outright fighting to hold on to a Best Bud is counterproductive. You're hurting yourself and her, and you're embarrassing your other friends and family.

4 Best Bud Britney

If there was a Best Bud award, you'd get it because you treasure your special bond and will do what it takes to keep it strong. That's what's so great about you and your Best Bud. You're both growing, independent-thinking girls who have the whole world ahead. And should one of you veer off course or stumble, the other one's always there by her side to advise and guide. What a ride for you and your Best Bud.

BEST BUD FACTORS

What Should You Know about the Best Bud?

A Best Bud is a good friend but one taken to the *n*th power. That's why both having a Best Bud and being one are so empowering—and so fun!

☑ Fact is, a Best Bud is an ideal and most precious friend. That means, she's a great chick just like you who knows that a close friendship is a gift and not something to be trashed or stepped on.

Me and Thea were Best Buds for three years. Almost inseparable. We vowed that we wouldn't change ever. But as soon as we hit high school, not only did we hardly ever talk, but she never called me. She was always on the phone with some junior girls. I tried to catch up with her and spend time, I instant messaged lots, but she acted cold. Actually she totally changed on me!

Josefina, 16

- ☑ Time sometimes puts a stress on Best Buds. It can really change things between girls, but that's just like other things in life.
- ☑ Sometimes Best Buds grow at different speeds. It's like flowers. Some grow to medium size, others to tall. Some blossom early and some wait until June to be in full bloom. And for some reason, some flowers sprout mainly thorns.

In seventh grade I tried to make a lot of new friends since I'd been sort of a nerd all through elementary school. I was constantly trying to be Best Buds with popular girls, especially Elodie. I hung out with her, wrote her nice notes, got her expensive birthday presents, and supported her. She said I was her very best bud. Next school year I wasn't in any of Elodie's classes. I tried to talk to her and she, like, totally ignored me. I felt completely and utterly rejected by her denial of our being buds. Now I was mud to her.

Fredericka, 16

- ☑ Sometimes even Best Buds can alter or falter along the road. They're human beings just like you. So don't be totally destroyed when your Best Bud changes. That's also part of being a Best Bud—understanding that as you both grow and change, your friendship will too.

FAST FRIEND MOVES

What You Should Do to Score a Best Bud

The basic steps to scoring a Best Bud are few in number—only three!—but they're etched in stone. You can't play around with them because they're key.

Here they are:

1. Keep your promises. Whatever you tell your Best Bud that you'll do, you must do.
2. Don't blab. Not even about little silly things—don't dish. When you're told something in confidence by your Best Bud or Buds, no matter whether it's something lame or juicy, lock the latest

buzz up into a safe place inside your brain. Don't take it out and show it off; don't even hint at it. A secret is something private, hidden, and concealed from others. So don't spill a secret ever, unless it's about something that's detrimental to your Best Bud, to yourself, or to other girls. If it's something really serious, you might want to tell a parent or another trusted adult so they can help fix whatever's wrong.

3. Be kind and caring. Care enough to do what it takes to keep your Best Buds your Best Buds. You see, Best Buds vary. Some need to vent fast, others need more of your time before they fill you in, and still others need you to help build up their self-esteem and compliment them. All need you to share their dreams and cheer them on. And no matter what, never, ever let jealousy or anything/anybody else come between you!

FIRST PERSON

How I Handled It–Jaclyn's Real-Life Story

It's funny how things seem so much clearer afterward, even if they appeared to be crystal clear at the time. Once I had a Best Bud, Pamela. People said we were inseparable. Really we almost had, like, a psychic connection—like we always knew what the other was thinking and we could finish each other's sentences. The weirdest thing of all was that we'd only known each other for a few months. But we felt like we'd been Best Buds since preschool. We got closer and closer even though we had lots of silly fights and would bicker like sisters. Finally, one of those little fights spelled the end for us.

I was certain it wasn't my fault. Sure it was Pam's. First thing she did was blow up at me online. I wasn't sure where all of the issues came from, but man! They came flying from all directions. Pam claimed I was never around and always too busy talking with other girls. I was shocked to hear this, so I typed back that I was tired of dealing with Pam's mood swings: "IF YOU DON'T STOP BEING BIPOLAR, LEAVE ME ALONE UNTIL YOU FIX YOUR MALFUNCTION!" I didn't really know what that meant, but it sounded way mature to me.

But even with all the cyber-yelling, I was sure it was just another one of the many teeny fights we'd had, and that we'd be able to work it out. Well, things didn't work out. The rift got bigger. Both of us started to build huge walls around ourselves. Sad to say, we said nasty things we didn't mean but the pain cut too deep. For her senior year, Pam transferred to another school and I dropped all my fave activities and just moped around the house. Often I'd pick up the phone to call Pam, then put it down. I even called her once and left her a message. But she never called me back.

So a silly little argument became a friend buster that destroyed the strongest friendship either of us had ever known. Two "best-est" buds were history.—Jaclyn, 18

CHICK-POINT
Grade the Girls
F ✱
D ✱✱
C ✱✱✱
B ✱✱✱✱
A ✱✱✱✱✱

Chick Grades:
–✱ for Pam
✱✱✱ for Jaclyn

Pam gets a minus-star, and you know why. She's done nothing positive or helpful since your close friendship broke up. She just picked up and went scat. She's probably sulking at this very moment. You, Jaclyn, get three stars. You've got the right idea, at least—that a Best Bud relationship's worth fighting for, every time. Proof is that you've tried to call Pam to talk things over and try to hash out your problem, if there even was one. So maybe you should try to call again?

Or what about sending a cute card that says, "Miss you. Can't we iron it out? Please, let's talk." That'll work.

Dear Diary

My Best Bud and I are like a diary to each other.

Annmarie, 14

Got your diary ready? Good! Find a clean sheet and copy this quote by George Eliot: *Best friend, my well-spring in the wilderness!*

Think about what this quote means and how it relates to you and to your Best Buds.

Friend Feelings

Now turn on your mental faucet and let it flow out—all your feelings about your best friend, your Best Bud. Write down what your Best Bud does for you and you for her; why she's so special to you and why you think you're so special to her. And write down what you two plan to do together tomorrow, next week, on your birthday or this summer.

You don't have a Best Bud?

Even better. Then you get to experience the exciting building of a Best Bud friendship now. How wonderful. What a thrill. And as with so many things, practice helps.

So, let's practice. How? Just choose a girl's name that you like, any girl's name, and write that name down. Then add an equal sign (=) and the words "My Best Bud." And then write down as plainly as you can what fun you and your Best Bud would have if she were real. What you'd tell her first off. What she'd tell you about next, and so on.

If she were a real live girl.

Guess what? She is real—you just haven't discovered her yet. But you will soon.

FRIEND SPOTTING

The Best Bud

The fab thing is that your future Best Bud is, at this very second, probably thinking about you and about how she wishes you two could form a close friendship.

So okay, all you have to do is be available. That means, you make sure you're capable of being a Best Bud.

How? By first watching some of the best Best Buds around. Do you know some girls who have a Best Bud or two, even though you're not one of them? If you do, observe them, just like you would observe other things. The weather, the ocean.

As soon as you observe these other tight friendships, you'll notice that when something super happens to one girl, she rushes over to tell her Best Buds *first.* Or when something bad happens, how her Best Buds cluster around her and tell her, "Hey, it's no big thing. Happens to everybody sometimes. We all mess up."

So, that kind of supportiveness is what you need to work on to be a Best Bud. You do that by thinking of the other girl first, by putting yourself in her place, and by being there for her—all the time. As she will be for you.

> My Best Bud reminds me of myself but just in a different and better way.
>
> Finley, 17

Yes, Best Buds do often resemble each other, not outwardly, but inside. You see the powerful potential in her, and at the same time, she recognizes you as who you really are—a great chick who's aiming high and exploring all her talents, little by little.

And you're not envious or jealous of her. And she's not jealous of you, either, because there's room for all the girl stars in the world.

> Envy and jealousy can destroy even the best of friendships. But only if you let them.
>
> Kendall, 15

So, hand in hand, heartwise, both of you climb up the ladder, in school, sports, your community, in your contributions to society. She's neither in front of you nor behind you, but steps upward and onward by your side. And if she should get ahead through extra hard work or circumstance, she'll stop and lend a hand and help you up too—just as you do her.

She's a terrific mind mate, your Best Bud is. She's someone you can tell whatever's on your mind and she won't laugh at you—and you do the same for her. She can talk to you without worrying about your reaction. And vice versa.

And the two of you can laugh with each other, not at each other. All the while she's your super soul supporter, and it feels way good to have her around, to touch base with her lots, to get her input, and to move ahead, shoulder to shoulder with her, to take on the world. Nothing can stop you two (or three or four, depending on how many Best Buds you have).

> But always remember, Best Buds being as terrific as they are, are something to really treasure.
>
> Faith, 14

Rx: Great Moves for Bagging a Best Bud and Being a Best Bud

Having a Best Bud isn't totally and absolutely essential, but it's such a wonderful and empowering thing to have one. Best news is, you can find a Best Bud wherever you are and whatever you do.

1. Be on the lookout for a Best Bud. Maybe among the friends you already have, one girl stands out. Talk with her more frequently to see how much you have in common.

   > I found my Best Bud in art class because we both love getting creative. You should see our mural, wow.
   >
   > Elisha, 15

2. But a Best Bud may also be among some new girls you'll meet, so don't limit yourself to your comfy circle of friends. Make new friends and see if one of those super chicks clicks especially with you. Some girls have found their Best Buds on the bus, while riding to school every morning or riding to a tennis match or on a field trip.

   > My Best Buds and I really bonded when we went on this class trip to Houston.
   >
   > Trinity, 16

My Best Buds and I have known each other for years. We go to the same synagogue and believe in the same God. But it wasn't until we did a big project together that we realized how close we really are.

Elise, 17

3. Be a Best Bud yourself. You do that by working on your Best Bud–ability, by being dependable and respectful and by keeping secrets. And your promises. And once you have one or more Best Buds, please hang on to them.

It all started with a boy I liked. So we went out, which seemed pretty simple. But then my longtime Best Bud Millie said she liked him and always had. I didn't know what to say besides mention the fact that Millie should've told me earlier. Millie got mad at me and I couldn't really do anything about it besides break up with the boy. But why? So Millie could go out with him? So I didn't do that and it was the end of our being Best Buds.

Casey, 18

4. Even longtime Best Bud relationships can be fragile, so you must guard against a breakup. You do that by talking—lots and lots of talking. Keeping your true feelings bottled up inside is never conducive to being Best Buds. Millie should've shared her real feelings about the boy early on, before Casey went out with him.

So, being Best Buds means revealing personal things about yourself to the other girl. Telling about your dreams, wishes, even your weaknesses.

If you mess up, and we all do sometimes, then apologize. Best Buds become even stronger friends each time one of them says "I'm so sorry" and the other says "Don't worry, it's okay." So, please don't ever delay saying you're sorry to your Best Bud.

My Best Bud and I had a horrible fight the other day. She called me all kinds of names and I did her too. Actually I was shocked about the

> language I used. That night I saw on the news that someone was hit by a car and killed. It was a hit and run, and it was a girl who had an argument at school and rushed out of the building, jumped in her car—and you know . . . So what I did was call Sema right away and apologize.
>
> Carolyne, 15

Chicks Mix

Oh, how powerful you feel when you have one or more Best Buds. And that power you feel is multiplied by the support you get from your Best Buds, and their empowerment is boosted by the support you give them. So, being Best Buds with a girl, or several, is like a boomerang. Not only does it help you to launch yourself to new heights and super sights, but it also comes back to you in many other positives.

Once you have managed to score one Best Bud, it'll be easier to score more. You can find them right under your nose or in any new fields you enter or in cyberspace.

Class Actions

You can find new Best Buds right under your nose. This year, as soon as school starts or a new class begins, try reaching out to some of the girls around you. Don't go around with a magnifying glass, giving every new girl a total head-to-toe chick checkup, but do go around with your ears wide open. If you hear a girl, any girl, chatting about something she likes and you like the same thing, speak up.

That means you have to know what you like.

Can you name five things that you really like? And five more things that are most important to you? Do that now. Then keep focusing your attention like a periscope on any girl, new to your crew or not, who seems to like or value the same things a lot.

Then, even better—what are some things you would like to know more about or to explore? New hobbies or styles or CDs or video games or TV shows you haven't watched but heard about?

Is there a girl anywhere on your radar screen who is into some of those things you are kinda curious about? Well, then, what about this? She'll talk to you about what she's into and you'll dish on stuff that she knows nothing about yet. Don't fret, before long you'll both be busy trying out for a new club or experimenting with a new eye shadow. Often Best Buds bond slowly, but once they do, how wonderful and strong that bond.

Chick-Mate

Your Best Buds are the perfect girlfriends for you, the ones who, of all the friends in your circle, are the nearest and dearest.

> My Best Bud. She's always, like, a huge part of my life. I can tell her my worst secrets and she tells me hers.
>
> Lauren, 14

- If you don't have a Best Bud yet, not to fear. She's out there. Just look more closely at all the great chicks you come in contact with each and every day. You see, she doesn't have a specific look or act in a certain way, but as a rule, she's no slouch and she's not a grouch.
- But you know what? A Best Bud can be as close as that friendly girl in Latin II class who sits a row over and chuckles at the same things you do. Or the girl in drama club who's so passionate when she paints the stage backdrops that she gets black streaks all over her white shirt.
- But hey, you don't even need school or a club meeting or a sports event to find a Best Bud. You can do it wherever you are by being Best Buds with the girls you know. Keep your promises. Be unselfish. Reveal your inner self—zits and all. Keep your lips zipped about any personal buzz that's shared with you in secret, and fight jealousness with all your power. When you make a mistake, just say "Oh, my gosh, I'm so sorry!"

Friendship Finder

Best Buds are most definitely a 9 or 10. As always, you make the final decision, so consult the Friendship Rating Scale.

FRIENDSHIP RATING SCALE

The Friendship Rating Scale goes from 1 to 10 (with 1 being way low and 10 being tops), which will help you make up your mind about which girls are hot friendship-wise and which for sure are not. You'll see a Friendship Rating at the end of each chapter!

1	Kick yourself for ever thinking about trying to be friends with her.
2	Serious waste of time.
3	May be a waste of time.
4	One more try can't hurt.
5	If you feel like investing more time, that's fine.
6	Keep trying to be her friend.
7	Try harder.
8	Try harder and smarter.
9	Put making friends with this girl on the top of your list.
10	Really strive to be friends with her. Then you will thrive.

Who ran to help me when I fell, and who would some pretty story tell, or kiss the place to make it well? My mother. Jane Taylor

Chapter 8

The Soul Pal

n., s.: The nonstop-there-for-you bud, 24/7, for real, always and forever, the never-quit bud, who brings out the best in you every second

Two girls were talking at a local mall restaurant and one said, "There is this man in South Africa who is fifty years old and still in close contact with every high school friend he ever had. I know about him because my friend is friends with his daughter. Can you imagine? Wonder how he's done that? How has he kept his friendships so strong and, like, forever? Isn't that amazing? That's what I'd like to do, but how?"

It certainly seems as if this man knows how to form forever friendships and make them last. Good for him. So let's learn from him not just what he's managed to do—keeping in touch with all his high school buds no matter where they ended up—but also how you can snag your own forever friends, and much easier, and in a much shorter time.

Actually just like *that,* with the snap of your fingers!

For your own forever friends are already here, with you. They're as close as they can get every day, every week, month, year. Forever, really. They're your true-until-the-end friends. And this is no joke. You have these dearest of friends all around you right now. Only one thing is missing: You just haven't realized their closeness. But once you do, you'll have a big *aha*! moment.

Recognizing your forever friends often starts with an *aha*!

It's so fab when you grasp this most wonderful fact, that your forever friends are like your Best Buds, only nonstop. You can be just about guaranteed that they'll never leave you. Never, ever. Unlike your other friends and even your Best Buds, some of who might move or change and lose their friend potential.

But that's not the case with your real and true forever friends, because they are your Soul Pals. And you will always have your soul, right? Just like your soul, your Soul Pals are an intricate part of you, or will be once you catch on and latch on to who they really are.

Until you do, just keep in mind that you will always, always have your Soul Pals. Day or night, rain or shine, for better or worse. No, for better and better!

How's that possible? you ask.

Read on!

What Makes Someone Your Soul Pal?

What makes a girl, or anyone else, your Soul Pal is some sort of connection from their soul to yours. And from yours to theirs!

Dear Dr. Erika:
Last week at school, the fire drill bell went off and our teacher hustled everyone outside to the grass slope that connects the buildings to the parking lot. And there we stood in groups after our teacher called roll to make sure we all made it.

That's, like, nothing unusual. We get those drills once every month, plus hurricane practices, plus other drills. Usually it's only a ten-minute interruption, then back to class. But it's always a nice break.

But this time we stayed and stayed out there and the buzz started. Reason was, two dozen cops pulled up. They had those ferocious German shepherd dogs and went through the building, like, with a fine-tooth comb. Then we had to step back from the building and we got real nervous. Some of the girls freaked out. Others got on their cells, called their moms, and they came and picked them up. But there was this one girl in my class who didn't act fidgety, not one bit. I'd noticed her before and thought she was cool. Was she ever. She found a bench and sat down, pulled out a book and read, calm as can be. Like she wasn't bugged-out at all. And before long, I sat next to her and we started talking, you know, about what she was reading and what I like to read. And other stuff, too, about what she did to unfreak herself in a scary situation and what I did. Things like that.

Ever since, we've chatted a bunch. We really have a gazillion things in common. This is so cool, how we're close now. A scare brought us together.

BTW, turned out, nothing was wrong at school that day. The cops just wanted those dogs to have a field exercise.

Christina, 16

FYI

Soul Pals have to do with your soul, and your soul is inside you—buried deep in your heart. You've never actually seen it, but it's there. It's what separates humankind from animals, some people say. Others call it the essence of a person, and still others describe the soul as the immortal core in all of us.

No matter how you define your soul, it's the part of you we're dealing with now. So how can you have a Best Bud with a soul-to-soul bond? We know that's tricky because we don't wear our souls on our sleeves. So, to form a friendship with someone that connects her with your soul, and you with hers, you have to pause and think a little.

Fact is, to find a Soul Pal, you may have to be a discoverer. Or an examiner or an explorer of your life as it is right now.

But what a wonderful process that is. To discover and examine something so extraordinary. For Soul Pals are the absolute fabbest friends. And like we said, what's so great about them is that you really do already have them. You just don't know it yet.

Fortunately, Madison does.

Freedom High School, USA

Sixth period is always so dull and draggy. It's the last period of the day and after all those busywork sheets and lectures and all that darn note taking, your hand cramps. And your back aches from those mountains of books you've lugged all day. Plus, your hair's gotten stringy and your crisp shirt's hot and clingy. Sure, you feel totally worn out by 2:15 P.M. But not today, thank goodness. Today's good.

As soon as Madison and her group get settled at their desks, they check the assignment posted on the board in their required keyboarding class, and there it is—a fun thing to do, for once.

The directions are for a project called *Create your own personal weekly schedule document.* The assignment is to fill in every hour and continue until four weeks are completed.

Madison waits for the teacher to take roll and explain in more detail what she wants the class to work on. Then she feels the corners of her mouth shoot up. The teacher just said, "You can work in groups if you want to."

Yes. As a bunch of girls roll their chairs over to form a circle around her, Madison gets back to adding data to the chart on her screen. A few more entries, then all done—ta-da. If asked, she'll help some of the other girls with this lesson, then maybe start on her calculus homework.

Not meant to be. Darn it. The girls have just scanned Madison's total weekly schedule, then glanced at her agenda for a whole month and found a typo. Or something.

"What's that supposed to mean?" one asks as she points to what Madison has filled in from 4:00 P.M. until 5:30 P.M. every Monday.

"Yeah, what's *MY T*?" another girl asks. "Are you taking a new class?"

Madison's already taking piano lessons, as well as playing on the tennis team and serving as a peer tutor every other Saturday. "No way," she says with a smile. "No more extra stuff for me; I got enough to do."

"So, what is it?"

"Well," Madison says, "if you guys really want to know . . ."

"Don't tell me, I got it. It's that new hottie, right? Mark Thomas."

"I bet it's some sort of code. It's turned around, right?" another girl chimes in. Madison explains what *MY T* means—"My Time."

"Your time?"

"Right. My Time. I get to chill out and do whatever I want. Just, like, sit around and listen to music. Or do my nails or take a nap. Sometimes I put on my rattiest outfit and fix popcorn and eat every kernel. Other times I take this long, perfumey bubble bath. . . ."

"Wow, what a great idea. To do, like, nothing? For a whole hour and a half? Way weird and totally terrif." The girls mob Madison but quietly and not so the teacher notices. "Can we come over sometime and do it with you?"

"Sure, anytime, just not on Mondays, okay?"

• • •

So, what is a Soul Pal? Something very, very special that can appear in three forms:

A Soul Pal can be a relative such as your mom, dad, siblings, or even cousins. A Soul Pal can be a friend with whom you've developed a very strong connection. And finally, and maybe most importantly, a Soul Pal can be YOU!

> My Soul Pal is so nice, kind, and caring that I can, like, bare my soul. He's my daddy.
>
> Kassie, 15

Second, a Soul Pal can appear in the form of your own soul, if you take time out to listen to your inner needs and honor your spirit.

> My true soul friend to the end is so reliable and with me around the clock, kind of like a best friend from birth. It's me.
>
> Teisha, 18

And finally, in your connection with what makes you really truly you. A Soul Pal exists in your connection with any girl who really gets the really, truly you. This kind of soul friendship is rare, let's face it, but it's out there, somewhere. It can happen, believe me. It can also include more than just the obvious!

So, how can you snag at least one Soul Pal?

By first and foremost eliminating everything that stands in the way of your finding your Soul Pal or pals and knowing that you're a girl with so much to offer the world. You've got to feel great about yourself! Otherwise, you'll just sabotage your Soul Pal possibilities.

Now let's find out what your true Soul Pal potential is.

FAST FRIENDSHIP FITNESS TEST

Are You a Good Soul Pal?

1 You're home alone for the first time in weeks. All your friends are on a school trip. Your parents are attending a late business meeting, and your little brother is staying next door at the neighbor's house. You:

a. Are terrified to be alone in the house. You grab your teddy bear, jump in bed, pull the covers over your head, and hide there until someone comes home.

b. Turn on all the lights, grab a big flashlight, and look under every bed, in every closet, behind the drapes. You pace from room to room, singing as loud as you can, banging pots and pans, to scare away any strangers. Alternately, you bark like a dog, arm yourself with a butter knife, and kick box.

c. Go through the student directory and call students you don't even know. Tell them to get their a— over here. It's an emergency. If that doesn't work, tell them it's an orgy. Somebody's bound to show up and you'll either bribe, browbeat, or threaten them into staying until your 'rents return.

d. Heave a sigh of relief. Ahh—home for once by yourself without anyone around to tell you what to do and when to do it. It's not that you don't like directions and even looking after your little brother, but to have some totally unspoken-for time is just fine with you. You have plenty to occupy you. You fix your fave snack and do your fave relax-to-the-max activity—maybe it's reading or writing or surfing the Net. Whatever it is, it's yours and yours alone!

2 Your younger sister has always been a pain. She whines and is way immature. Any little thing not going her way makes her either scream out loud or boo-hoo. Actually, she's just jealous of you because you're older and winning all these awards. Now Mom's going to Seattle for a week, and the sitter's the kind who wants you to handle everything. You:

a. Fall apart. Totally. How can you be expected to keep everything going when your little sis is so hard to handle even with Mom home? With her gone, this is going to be a nightmare. This is freak-out time.

b. Worry a bunch long before Mom's even left, also while she's gone, and after she returns. Actually you know you can keep things going fine—well, maybe? Probably?—but what're you going to do if that little brat has one of those incredible screaming fits? You don't know, but you figure that if you worry over every detail, you will be prepared for whatever happens. So you pace and ponder, worry and wonder. You read up on child rearing and wish you could e-mail Dr. Spock.

c. Make sure your little sis knows exactly who the boss is. You do this by stencilling some tough rules on the kitchen wall: "1. No whining or no supper! 2. Not one darn tear, you hear?! 3. If you act like a baby, it's off to bed and no maybe!" Then you follow the little pest wherever, keeping very close watch. That's the way to nip any childish behavior in the butt—I mean, bud! You run a tight ship. Mom could learn from you.

d. Sit down with your sib and explain what a great opportunity this is. Let's make Mom proud, okay? Then for each day that runs smoothly, you'll reward your sis with something fun you do together. By the end of the week, you'll be friends, close friends, maybe even super Soul Pals.

3 Your parents have started changing the subject whenever you walk into the room. And that's not what they usually do. So, you know something is going on, but when you ask them what's up, they say nothing, then change the subject fast. You:

a. Think that they're discussing you. Sure, they're supremely disappointed in you. And no wonder. You really are a dud, just really not good at anything, just a total failure, so why even try?

b. Try to find out what they're talking about. But all you hear is a phrase or two and your name. You guess it's all about that C-plus you made last week. They're worried that you won't get into a good college even though that's four years away. Better plan on an alternate career, such as animal-toenail technician.

c. Creep around the foundation of your house to get to the open window of the room they're having the discussion in. When that doesn't work and you ruin the prize peonies plus pick up some poison ivy, you install a mommy-and-daddy cam. Only too bad the battery is low, but maybe if you "borrow" the voice-activated tape recorder from school, you'll get somewhere. Nobody, but nobody's gonna keep you out of the loop!

d. Politely ask your parents what's going on. They finally admit that they're discussing what to get you for your birthday. You love surprises, so you stop being nosy right away. Plus, you know that whatever it'll be, it's going to be something totally fabulous. Your 'rents are super. You love them; they are the best.

4 You and the other members of your journalism club are brainstorming. One girl suggests doing a feature on how girls can be better friends to themselves—and how they can use their girl power to change the world. The majority thinks it's a good idea, and the adviser tells everyone to do some interviews. You:

a. Think it's a great idea, but you're worried that other girls will think it's stupid. So, you sidle up to a girl in the bathroom and timidly ask her the first question from your list: *Can a girl be a good friend to herself?* She looks at you like you have three heads and snaps "No!" and turns away. You hurry out of the bathroom with your head down. Maybe this assignment wasn't a great idea after all.

b. Do some research on the Net to get started, but you're really afraid that people will think the idea is weird and make fun of you for it. You couldn't take the teasing. So, instead of interviewing other girls, you make up answers that you think they would say. Your adviser will never find out, and this saves you any embarrassment. Anyway, it's just easier to make something up.

c. Track down the meanest chicks in school, tail them as they skip class, and offer them a cool deal: You won't turn them in if they give you an interview. When they laugh in your face, you stomp to the office and report that some girls in the back of the gym are acting very, very unfriendly.

d. Survey your friends and classmates about how they think girls can be better friends to themselves, and write the best paper ever on your findings. You're surprised at how interested girls are about this subject. Turns out that your article inspires lots of girls and soon everyone is talking about this hot topic. And who knows? Oprah Winfrey might hear about your research and invite you and a few of your best pals to appear as guests. She might even give you a car to share!

Now it's time to find out your FQ: Tally your answers. How many A's, B's, C's, and D's do you have?

3 or 4 A's, check out Answer 1.
3 or 4 B's, check out Answer 2.
3 or 4 C's, check out Answer 3.
3 or 4 D's, check out Answer 4.

If you have a mixture of A's, B's, C's, and D's, look at all the answers. Obviously, there's a bit of everything in you, which is fab. Now, can you work on having a little less of the Answer 1 attitude and a little more of the Answer 4 attitude?

Answers

1 Sobby Bobbie

It's okay to be shy and nervous. Most of us are at some time. But if you always scurry off and withdraw into your shell, you won't achieve what you're meant to—great things. So next time you face a challenge, take a deep breath, stand your ground, and face it—with your chin up. You can handle any problem that comes along, or get help if the problem's too big to handle. But always know, you really can do it.

2 Lame Dame

You are on the right track, and that's just great. Now all you have to do is stay on track. So stop always wavering like a waif. You're a smart girl, so stop second-guessing yourself. All that time you put into being a worrywart is much better spent being steadfast and following through with what's in your heart. And that is that you want to succeed. And you will, once you commit yourself to your task.

3 Bulldozer Rose

You care so much and have lots of compassion. That's wonderful. Now, the only thing you need to do is get your directions straight. Always running and blindly gunning backfires on you. From now on, slow down until you have clearly thought about your goal, then go for the gold.

4 One Terrific Chick

What a mature approach and top attitude you have. Always. You know just when to take charge and when to follow someone else's lead, and these talents will come in handy later in life. Of course, you aren't perfect—who is?—but you're perfectly fabulous in the way you analyze and size up a situation and then give it your best effort. You really are one terrific chick! What a self-realized girl you are. What a dear friend to yourself, your friends, and your family. Wow!

SOUL PAL FACTORS

What Should You Know about the Soul Pal?

A Soul Pal is similar to a soul model and soul mate. But while a soul model is a special role model and a soul mate is a life partner, a Soul Pal is like the very, very, very best friend you can have.

- ☑ This type of friend is extraordinary because this is a pal whose connection to you goes way beneath any surface. Fact is, the Soul Pal bond reaches inside you and touches the inner you—in other words, your spirit—and forms a soul bond. And this soul bond accesses what makes you you. What makes you so special.
- ☑ Therefore, the Soul Pal bond is the most profound and most beautiful relationship you can have at this point in your life. And, wow, is it ever empowering. With a Soul Pal, you can always count on your soul being at peace. Because a Soul Pal is a soul soother, a solace giver, and a heart healer.
- ☑ By being a great friend to yourself, you'll always have a Soul Pal around—you! And you'll also have your girl Soul Pals and your family to help you along. So, you're always doing fine.

No matter what, I can always depend on my mom. She lets me tell her everything that's on my mind. It always makes me feel better.

Keila, 16

- ☑ But sometimes you can get in such a rush and have so many competing ideas and conflicting thoughts on your mind that they overwhelm how you're feeling about yourself. It's all too easy to go from feeling great to feeling grumpy. And sometimes it's easier to think about the bad things rather than focusing on the good. So, how can you keep your relationship with yourself strong?
- ☑ First of all, take a break. Look at the sky, the trees, the myriad colors of flowers. Take the time to notice the little things around you and pay attention to how they make you feel. You'll be surprised that just looking around you with an open heart can give you power. You are so special, wonderful, and you have the whole world at your fingertips. So be happy with yourself, be at peace, and be filled with excitement about your great friends and your great future.
- ☑ Know this: There's never any delay when you reach inside yourself and draw on your own strength, your own power, and your dearest friends' power and support. With your close circle of friends around you, your potential will be truly unlimited.

FAST FRIEND MOVES

What You Should Do to Score a Soul Pal

1. Think about your family, whether it's the typical collection of mom, dad, kids, dog, cat, and goldfish or not. But really, among your relatives you can definitely find a Soul Pal. Why? Because you have common roots and because family is so user-friendly. You get to see some of them almost every day. So choose your mom, dad, sis, bro, cousin, aunt, unc, gran, or gramps as your super Soul Pal. And know they have your best interests at heart. Yes, family members are some of the best Soul Pal material you'll ever find. Why? Because they have a history with you, like the old friends, and an affection connection, like close friends. And they love you! So they have double or triple the potential as Soul Pals.

2. Be your own best Soul Pal, which is easy. All you have to do is decide to do it. Decide to form a strong Soul Pal friendship with yourself. You start by meeting yourself. Stop what you're doing and shake hands with yourself now. And as you do, say, "Hi there, glad to meet you, ________. (Fill in your name.)" Think about all of the things that you love and enjoy. Think about what makes you specially, uniquely you. It may sound silly, but have you ever tried it? Have you ever looked inside yourself and seen all the beauty, the talent, and the unlimited potential that're there in abundance? Have you ever stopped to celebrate your fabulous heart, your incredible spirit, and your wonderful soul?
3. Think of you in the future. Picture yourself already having realized your dreams and being happy and productive. Hold that vision in front of your inner eye. Then file it away to be pulled up again anytime you need it. You aren't just the product of your past and present work and hopes, you are also the product of what a great person you have the potential to become.

So bring out, and cling to, the best view of you.

Also memorize a meaningful phrase, quotation, or verse you've read that uplifts you and inspires you, and repeat it often to yourself whenever you need or want to.

FIRST PERSON

How I Handled It-Kirby's Real-Life Story

Last Thursday when I came home from school, Mom was there, which was not the usual routine. Usually Mom comes in at 7 P.M.

"Everything okay?" I asked, after putting my book bag down.

"Sure," Mom said. "I just needed to take off early." I noticed that she looked super tired.

"Oh no, are you feeling bad again?" I asked. Mom's been having a lot of migraines in the last few days.

My mom sighed and said, "Kirby, just promise me one thing. Whatever you do, don't work in a bank."

My mom used to love her job at the bank, but ever since she got this new boss, she's been really stressed out and tired. We used to be really close, but now we hardly get to spend time together like we used to. Mom looked so sad and tired and I realized something—I missed spending time with her. Then I got the greatest idea.

"Tell you what, Mom. Why don't you rest for an hour? I'll clean up, do laundry and stuff. Then I'll take you out to eat. Just the two of us, okay? Like a girls' night out."

Mom's eyebrows shot up but she wasn't angry, only caring: "Did you fail another physics test? Hmmmm?"

"Nope, made the second best grade in class. Plus, I saved some cash from my last babysitting gig. So, any restaurant you like."

Mom was touched but still she said, "No, let's forget about it. You need your money. I know about those highlights you want in your hair for the prom—"

"That can wait. Now, go on, lie down."

I was just finishing up in the kitchen when the phone rang. It was Sydney, one of my friends. "Hey, can I pick you up in a sec? My dad can drop us off at the mall while he's going to Home Depot. So, we can, like, grab a latte, then pop into Borders and take a peek at the new *Jane* mag."

"Gee, wish I could," I said. "But I've already got something planned. Can we maybe do it later this week?"

I went to change into a pair of dressy pants and a cute top and get ready for my girls' night out.

And Mom and I went to a great restaurant where we talked and talked. Felt like we were sisters, you know, two females, separated by twenty-five years but not by much of anything else.—Kirby, 16

Chick Grades: ✱✱✱✱✱

Kirby gets five stars with all the super plusses she wants. Her mom came first, Kirby knew. After all, she was Kirby's Soul Pal. Staying connected to one's Soul Pal is always a top goal. Soul Pals rule!

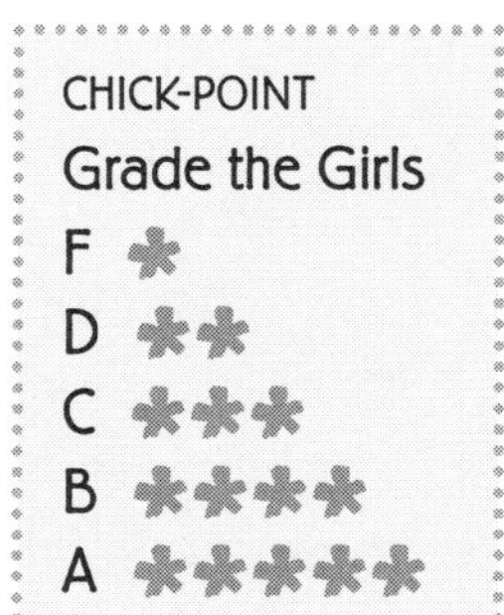

My mom's my deep-down best pal. She doesn't waste her time screaming and accusing me. But yet she helps me in choosing the right thing to do. Every time.

Hannah, 17

Dear Diary

Wow, your diary is probably waaay full by now! Find three blank sheets of paper. On the first one write "Family." Then list all your relatives and indicate what you have in common with them. Or not. Write freely, just whatever comes to mind. Then zoom in on one or two family members, the ones you feel closest to. The ones you sense you can always turn to when in hot water, or not. And then write a paragraph detailing how you could turn these special relatives into your Soul Pals. What can you do to make it clear to them just how much they mean to you?

Head up the second sheet with the word "Me." Then describe yourself in the most glowing terms. Tell all about how wonderful you are. Exaggerate if you want; use the most superlative of superlatives, but don't even think of writing down anything negative. Not one word. That would be like looking at an award-winning rose and saying, "Man, what a yucky collection of thorns!" You see, you are flawless just the way you are because you're looking into your heart and soul and writing all about the greatness that resides in there. That makes you smart, fabulous, beautiful, brave, nice, independent thinking, and powerful. In short, a girl who will accomplish so much in this world. Wow, what a terrific Soul Pal you are to yourself.

On the last sheet, write your own cheer. Yay, let's hear it for me! The cheer can be any collection of words that suits you. It can be a series of the most beautiful words you know or something simple like "I promise myself to do my best" or "I have great plans for my future" or "I will make a difference."

Then make copies of it, plaster one on your bathroom mirror, put a copy in your book bag, another under your pillow. Think of this as your password to the one all-powerful Soul Pal who's always, always happy to hear from you!

Of course, if there's a girl in your world who is soul-connected to you, tell her all about it.

FRIEND SPOTTING

The Soul Pal

The Soul Pal is what makes your life totally wonderful because when you have a Soul Pal, or several, you stand out. You feel protected at all times; you're simply stronger. And when you're stronger, everything else seems way easier. So, make sure you have a Soul Pal or two or three.

☑ You can find your Soul Pals right in your home. Just take a special look at all the members of your family. Which one or which ones do you feel closest to? Don't make judgments about the ones you don't feel particularly close to. This is no time to find fault. You just want to discover the one or two or three relatives you have who are on your side always. Even if you bare your darkest secrets to them, they will still love you unconditionally. Those are your Soul Pals. Respect them, rejoice in them, and love them back.

My sister's the one who's always there when I need someone to listen. And she can keep huge secrets. Actually I trust her with my life.

Michelle, 17

☑ Look in the mirror now and smile, for the girl looking back at you is another top Soul Pal. And she'll never leave you, so treat her well. Spoil her whenever you can. If she has special interests, indulge her. Paint with her. Let her flip through those free travel brochures of Prague or Portugal. Write away and get those college pamphlets for her. Plan to take her to a special chick flick. Let her read some chick lit. Play her favorite CDs, or sing for her, with her. Yes, I know I'm acting as if you and your Soul Pal were separate. Sometimes you need to step back to truly appreciate your inner Soul Pal. Do so now.

☑ Finally, make the tie to your forever Soul Pal as strong as you can. That means, you need to take the time to think about what a Soul Pal is and then spend time with her; that means yourself and/or the person(s) who you feel soul-connected to.

So, every week, just take a few minutes to check in with your soul, your spirit. And with any family members and girls whom you feel a deep connection to, soulwise.

Rx: Great Moves for Finding Soul Pals

1. Reach your arms skyward now and know that you can have it all—all the best Soul Pals you want. They're just waiting for you. So take the first step and today be especially friendly to the various members of your family. Surprise them with a nice note, a small gift, a little pesky chore done just for them. Fix dinner even when it isn't your turn. You're a super chick, so sure, you can fix some super chick salad, chick soup, or a chick filet sandwich for everyone.
   Or open a new recipe book and chick it all out.
2. Talk to yourself and tell yourself what a most terrific chick you are. Yes, you are a strong and heroic chick, and now you have lots of friends, beginning with yourself.
3. Don't always just be busy-busy-busy. Now and then schedule some free time, some me-time. Just sit with the TV off, your cell off, the radio/CD player off. All quiet on your home front, okay? Let the stillness fill you. And let your mind go free, let it roam, let it light on any thought it wants to. Let your soul sing.

Your best friends and you can make the most beautiful music by being there for one another, encouraging one another, cheering one another on, and striding powerfully, shoulder to shoulder, out into this wonderful world.

Only one more thing left to do—and that is to have a reality chick.

Chick-Mate

This reality chick requires one thing.

> To make some really terrif friends, you gotta be a really terrific chick. And that means never stop working on yourself. Make yourself grow more.
>
> Annya, 18

So, to get all the fab friends, Best Buds, and Soul Pals you want, don't sit back and wait around.

Get out and about. Get involved, get busy. Redo your room, ride your bike, garden, and maybe make some cyberpals—as opposed to cyberbullies.

And as often as you can, walk, and as you walk, pick up trash. Makes you feel good to do something for our beautiful Earth.

Then bake your mean caramel cake. Eat one slice and take the rest to the old woman across the street who's been waiting for her grandson to come home from Iraq.

And chick out books—oh, wonderful books! They're filled with thoughts that touch you, move you, and inspire you to aim higher. Read great poems. Ask the librarian for recommendations. Also, fill your heart with nature's most amazing sights and sounds. Imagine the swell of a wave and the crashing of the ocean against some stark cliffs. Envision the mountains in the distance, bathed in pink light. Look at a night sky and drink in the vast stillness.

Remember all the heartwarming stories of courage you've heard, and give thanks that you are alive in this wonderful day and age. That you're a top chick right now. Say thank you several times a day, to your parents, to yourself, and to anyone else who made it all possible.

To have great Soul Pals, you must be a great Soul Pal. What an overwhelming feeling for you, when you have discovered that.

FRIENDSHIP RATING SCALE

The Friendship Rating Scale goes from 1 to 10 (with 1 being way low and 10 being tops), which will help you make up your mind about which girls are hot friendship-wise and which for sure are not. You'll see a Friendship Rating at the end of each chapter!

Friendship Finder

Soul Pals are most definitely a 10-plus or an 11 on your trusty Friendship Rating Scale.

1	Kick yourself for ever thinking about trying to be friends with her.
2	Serious waste of time.
3	May be a waste of time.
4	One more try can't hurt.
5	If you feel like investing more time, that's fine.
6	Keep trying to be her friend.
7	Try harder.
8	Try harder and smarter.
9	Put making friends with this girl on the top of your list.
10	Really strive to be friends with her. Then you will thrive.

And we find at the end of a perfect day the soul of a friend we've made. Carrie Jacob Bond

Chapter 9

The Fast Fab Friend and Best Bud Finder

The Chick List

Now that you've become an expert on friends, you know that finding fab friends and Best Buds is way crucial right now.

> *Actually, friends are worth more than silver or platinum.*
>
> *Jennifer, 17*

And friend finding has only three parts to it.

1. First, you must ditch all the unfriendly girls in your life. Make them gone. Out of there! Ciao, au revoir. That includes all the girls who are friendship-challenged—from milder forms to the most severe, okay?—and also those who act flat-out like your worst enemies. Until these types of girls change, just tell them bye, see ya—not! and move on.
2. Next, jump boldly into the vast friendship pool that stretches all around you, meet as many nice girls as you can, and start being their friend. Just talk to them, say something nice, keep talking, and spend time with them doing fun activities. Or studying. Or dishing about guys, whatever.

3. Then become Best Buds with one, two, or three top chicks and form strong bonds with them. Share a secret with them and keep mum about theirs. Finally discover your true Soul Pals.

So, now you know how to have a bunch of fab friends and Best Buds. And how to disarm the mean girl swarm. Wow, I'm so proud of you.

Below is a great and quick chick list to remind you of your friendship-making powers as you now soar ahead in the world—with smarts and style.

The Fab Friend Chick List

Directions: Please place checks next to those items you feel very confident about. Each check is worth 10 points.

1. ___ Can you identify the Airhead in your school or group and not have your life be affected by her?
2. ___ Can you spot the Me-Me Chick(s) and not let her super selfishness rub off on you?
3. ___ Can you recognize the Phony and not be taken in by her baloney?
4. ___ Do you know who the Enemy and the Frenemy are and can you protect yourself from them?
5. ___ Do you have at least a few fab friends, or more?
6. ___ Do you have at least one Old Friend that you keep up with?
7. ___ Do you have at least one Study Buddy?
8. ___ Do you have at least one Boy Bud?
9. ___ Do you have at least one Best Bud?
10. ___ Do you know who your Soul Pals are?

Very Best Wishes to You!

Bye for now, girl. You're almost there!

Yes, you're really well on your way. Just remember this: The whole world is your friend, the girl world especially, and you can reach out. In the vast ocean of great girls and supernice chicks, you can find many, many you'd like to spend time with.

Then do it.

Next, from the many, many great girls and supernice chicks, you can pick and choose a few that you can develop a closer friendship with. A dearer relationship that shows you dare, you can share, and you really care.

Now you know how, you can do it—all you have to do is try.

From those few great and super chicks, soon one or two Best Buds will evolve and emerge—with all of you giving and taking.

And then more and more wonderful things will happen. You will make great friends, fab friends, forever friends who touch your soul, and your very best buds. And while you do this, remember you already have, right now, this very moment, the very best and forever perfect bud already. And that is YOU—wonderful and powerful you!

So, onward with your wonderful life, your golden dreams, and your high hopes—you, surrounded by all your fab friends, Best Buds, and your forever friends, will shine and climb, yes. You will win and work wonders.

Yes, you, all of you, will feel so alive. You will get so much done, have so much fun, and the world will be better.

Go ahead and be what you're meant to be—powerful, peaceful, and purposeful.

Appendix

Fab and Cool Chick Tools

This section offers a selection of the latest and coolest print materials plus Internet resources specifically designed to lend you a hand as you make lots more friends.

Friendly Girl Guides and Teen Zines

***Girls' Life* magazine**
4517 Hartford Road
Baltimore, MD 21214
www.girlslife.com

***Seventeen* magazine**
1440 Broadway
13th Floor
New York, NY 10018
www.seventeen.com

YM
G&J USA Publishing
375 Lexington Avenue
New York, NY 10017
www.ym.com

Teen People
P.O. Box 999
Radio City Station
New York, NY 10101
www.teenpeople.com

CosmoGIRL!
224 West 57th Street
New York, NY 10019
www.cosmogirl.com

Teen Vogue
Condé Nast
4 Times Square
New York, NY 10013
www.teenvogue.com

Friendly Chick Books

The Care and Keeping of Friends (American Girl Library Series) by Sally Seamans, Nadine Bernard Westcott (Illustrator), Pleasant Company Publications, 1996

The Girls' Book of Friendship: Cool Quotes, True Stories, Secrets and More by Catherine Dee, Little Brown and Co., 2001

The Girls' Guide to Friends: Straight Talk for Teens on Making Close Pals, Creating Lasting Ties, and Being an All-Around Great Friend by Julie Taylor, Three Rivers Press, 2002

A Smart Girl's Guide to Friendship Troubles (American Girl Library Series) by Kelley Patti Crisswell, Angela Martini (Illustrator), Pleasant Company Publications, 2003

Teen Girlfriends: Celebrating the Good Times, Getting Through the Hard Times (Girlfriends Series) by Julie DeVillers, Carmen Renee Berry (Introduction), Wildcat Canyon Press, 2001

The Truth About Girlfriends (*Seventeen*) by Amy Fishbein, HarperCollins Publishers, 2001

Friendly Chick Sites

www.freshangles.com—A teen e-zine.

www.cyberteens.com—A site with several areas of interest.

http://education.indiana.edu/cas/adol/adol.html—Adolescence Directory On-Line, a service of Indiana University. Has many links to other sites.

http://dir.yahoo.com/Society_and_Culture/Cultures_and_Groups/teenagers/girls/Magazines/

Yahoo.com's links to teen e-zines. This list has something for pretty much every interest.

www.gurl.com—Gurl.com has many areas of interest for teenage girls.

I felt so lonely, scared, and helpless before I found some friends. Now, what a difference. I'm happy each and every day. Peace to all the girls in the world.

Bianca, 17

Index

M

N

O

P

R

S